To our readers

Peter Ralston

Going There

Sometimes you've just got to go there. The insightful journals kept by our Island Fellows and published in these pages, for example, are a direct result of "going there" — first-hand experience is what the Island Institute's fellowship program is all about, and the journals reflect it. Likewise, when Ben Neal, a member of the Institute staff, had the opportunity to spend ten days aboard the National Marine Fisheries Service's research vessel ALBATROSS, the opportunity for a fish-by-fish account of his experience was irresistible.

Two other stories this year have to do with the Arctic and efforts to go there: Donald MacMillan's pioneering 1925 expedition to northern Greenland, and the globe-girdling research vessel TURMOIL's trip to Iceland in the summer of 2000. Seventy-five years of invention and technological advance have made Arctic travel a lot easier, but they have not minimized the importance of that region's connections to the rest of the world, or the need to go there to learn its secrets.

Artists such as Andrew and Jamie Wyeth have gone to Maine islands for most of their lives, each extracting very different visions from his island travels.

"Going there" need not always mean a trip in the literal sense: from fragmentary accounts a historian paints a vivid picture of events he could never have seen; from interviews with fishermen who once relied on a lost technology to support their families, a gifted seamstress creates a magnificent quilt that tells their story; in her mind, a writer asks whether the space she "shares" with a long-departed family is somehow sacred. These are virtual journeys, and they are no less valid than actual trips across the expanses of our planet.

Exploration is at the heart of this year's *Island Journal*, and this theme reflects our deeply-held belief that only by constantly exploring — literally or through the imagination — can we hope to understand a world whose future health and very existence could depend on what we learn.

The Editors

ISLAND JOURNAL

The Annual Publication of the Island Institute
Volume Eighteen

page 6

page 26

page 12

page 34

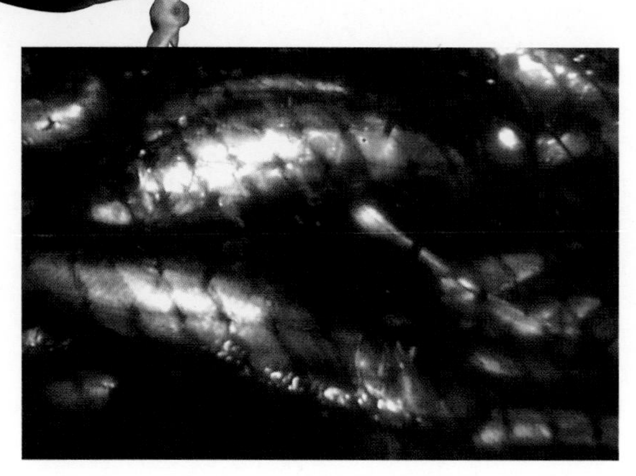

page 20

Cover: Peter Ralston

page 62

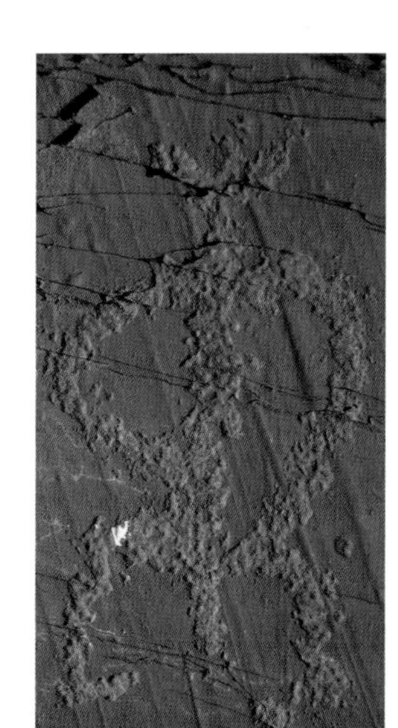

page 76

page 93

page 88

page 83

Serving the Islands and Communities of the Gulf of Maine

ISLAND JOURNAL

PUBLISHER
Philip W. Conkling

EDITOR
David D. Platt

ART DIRECTOR
Peter Ralston

COPY EDITOR
Esme McTighe

GRAPHICS RESEARCH
Jessica Baines

DESIGN & PRODUCTION
Michael Mahan Graphics
Bath, Maine

PRINTING
J. S. McCarthy / Lettersystems
Augusta, Maine

ISLAND INSTITUTE

PRESIDENT
Philip W. Conkling

EXECUTIVE VICE PRESIDENT
Peter Ralston

CHIEF OPERATING OFFICER
Josée L. Shelley, CPA

EXECUTIVE ASSISTANT
Judy Tierney

PERSONNEL & OPERATIONS DIRECTOR
Marianne H. Pinkham

OFFICE AND PERSONNEL ASSISTANT
Kathy Allen

MIS SUPPORT PROVIDER/DATA BASE MANAGER
Richard L. Davis

OFFICE AND OPERATIONS COORDINATOR
Karen L. Hansen

RECEPTIONIST
Tammy Hamel

FINANCE MANAGER
Joann S. King

COMMUNITY INITIATIVES DIRECTOR
Stefan Pakulski

COMMUNITY INITIATIVES COORDINATOR
Susan Valaitis

ISLAND SCHOOLS COORDINATOR
James C. Doyle

FELLOWSHIP COORDINATOR
Sandra H. Thomas

MAINE CONSERVATION CORPS VOLUNTEER/ COMMUNITY INITS. ASST.
Beth Nelson

MARINE RESOURCES ASSOCIATE
Leslie Fuller

MARINE RESOURCES OUTREACH COORDINATOR
Benjamin Neal

VESSEL OPERATIONS/ SEA STATION FIELD MANAGER
Corrie Roberts

INFORMATION DIRECTOR
David D. Platt

PUBLICATIONS ASSOCIATE
Charles G. Oldham

PUBLICATIONS MARKETING ASSOCIATE
Mike Herbert

GIS PROJECT MANAGER
Chris W. Brehme

GIS ANALYST
Andy Boyce

WEBMASTER
Chris Broadway

COMMUNICATIONS/ PUBLIC RELATIONS DIRECTOR
Linda Cortright

MEMBERSHIP COORDINATOR
Jody A. Herbert

MEMBERSHIP DEVELOPMENT ASSISTANT
Kathy Estabrook

RETAIL STORE MANAGER
Jin Lawrence

RETAIL STORE ASSISTANT MANAGER
Leah Fitz-Gerald

TEMPORARY POOL
Emily Allen, Anne Baldridge, Kate Griffin, Faith Rainbolt, Marcia Reisman, Pat Ritchie, Jessica Stearns, Sally Thibault

Peter Ralston

FROM THE HELM

PHILIP W. CONKLING

The view from the fourth floor at Institute's new headquarters at 386 Main Street extends from the edge of the view from the fourth floor at the Island Institute's new headquarters at 386 Main Street extends from the edge of Rockland Harbor over West Penobscot Bay to the long, low shorelines of Vinalhaven and North Haven. Beyond them, the high mass of Isle au Haut is visible as well. To the south, past Owls Head, Matinicus and Criehaven lie like faint lines on the horizon, and at night the light at Matinicus Rock flickers in the sky. To the north, over the Rockland breakwater, you can just make out the small islands at the southern tip of the Islesboro chain. It is tempting to imagine climbing onto the roof of the building to gaze even further, east and west to the islands off Mount Desert and the island kingdoms of Casco Bay — or even further east to Cutler and West Quoddy Head, or westward to Cape Porpoise and the Knubble off York Harbor. Sometimes it is gratifying to be reminded how vast is the essential character of the islands and coastline of the Gulf of Maine, a place that can be viewed as a whole only from the distance of space, though never encompassed nor fully appreciated in the span of a single life.

Down on the first floor the Institute's new store, Archipelago, has the space to feature the work of island artisans from the length and breadth of Maine. The new exhibit space adjacent to the store has invited many new friends in the front door to make common cause with our passion for this en-isled and watery region. In between the first and fourth floor, a few dozen staff members work tirelessly on projects that range in scale from an island's one-room schoolhouse to the mysterious migrations of sea creatures throughout the Gulf of Maine. Many of these efforts took a quantum leap forward with the establishment of the Island Fellows Program that places young people, fresh out of college or graduate school, in challenging real-life work assignments in remote island and coastal communities. Being able to view the region at different scales simultaneously is one of the hallmarks of the Island Institute's approach to the issues that surround and sometimes confound us all.

Like any vital enterprise, we constantly ask ourselves not only what is working in our projects, but also what and how we can do better. And of those things that have been done well, is there someone else, ideally closer to the community or the issue in question, who can continue the work while we move to chart new territory or test new approaches? We should always be asking ourselves which programs we are uniquely qualified to continue, which ones we might encourage others to take on for themselves. A review of last year's work presents some clear answers to these questions.

Four of the largest island projects in which the Institute played an important role during the past year — on Frenchboro, North Haven, Vinalhaven and Long Island — share common themes, though the challenges and circumstances differed in each. Frenchboro faced the sale of a single piece of property that encompassed over half of the community. Developing the property would have changed the island forever. North Haven struggled with the need for a strategic vision for a community future, encompassing the disparate and sometimes disagreeing spectrum of its residents. Vinalhaven had a grand plan for a performing arts center and library at a new island school that substantially exceeded the amount of money state and local tax support could raise. And Long Island, Maine's newest island community, had a plan to build a handsome town library.

The staff at the Institute work from a long-range plan that sets annual priorities. Interestingly, none of the projects above appeared on our annual plan, either because no one had anticipated their timing, or because we had not been specifically asked by islanders to participate. Regardless, the projects began to hit like a chain reaction, and we were able to respond to each in turn. Frenchboro, in a $3 million campaign, was able not only to purchase the 950 acres that had been put on the market, but also packaged its conservation plan as a community revitalization program to renovate its historic one-room school, as well as its church, parsonage and library. North Haven residents coalesced around a $2.7 million Waterman's Community Center proposal to renovate a historic gateway building at the head of the ferry landing into a community center and performing arts space. The Town of Vinalhaven, along with its nonprofit arm, Partners in Island Education, undertook a $2 million private fundraising effort to complement state and local funds and guarantee the construction of an expanded school library and the island's first ever performing arts center. Finally, Long Islanders raised over $600,000 of the $850,000 they need for their first free standing town library, replacing what has heretofore been confined to the basement of the schoolhouse.

Being able to view the region at different scales simultaneously is one of the hallmarks of the Island Institute's approach to the issues that surround and sometimes confound us all.

All of these projects were accomplished by developing and facilitating key partnerships to keep projects going when the going got rough. On Frenchboro, the Institute worked with town fathers (and mothers), the Maine Coast Heritage Trust and the Maine Seacoast Mission to strategize the interlocking elements of the plan. On North Haven, we worked with the Arts and Enrichment Council and with members of the town government and school board to shape the community center plan. On Vinalhaven, the selectmen and school board authorized the private fundraising undertaken by Partners in Island Education, and the Island Institute helped develop the case statement for prospective funders. On Long Island, the crucial first dollars for the library came from $32,000 in tax revenues from hard-working islanders, while the Institute contributed small grants and helped with introductions and letters of support to private foundations. Collectively these projects add up to an unprecedented new investment in Maine island communities.

The projects share key ingredients. All were first envisioned by the islanders themselves and were energized when the islanders reached off-island for extra help — often to complete the final pieces. In addition to the hundreds and hundreds of private individual contributions from islanders, summer residents and on-island organizations, each of these projects benefited enormously from the support of a new source of corporate funding. MBNA and the people of MBNA who contribute to its foundation have become a source of philanthropic partnership that was almost unimaginable a few years ago. The MBNA Foundation has established a school grants program that accepts proposals from all 14 island schools. MBNA's Library Grants Program has been the largest source of library funding among the island libraries since Andrew Carnegie's library building program a century ago.

Turning to the larger scale of the Gulf of Maine where the Institute is also active, last year marked another kind of turning point. For the first time ever, key groups in Maine's disparate marine community came together to compete successfully for $6.7 million in federal funding to create the Gulf of Maine Ocean Observing System (for more on GOMOOS, see page 31 of this issue). GOMOOS represents a unique collaboration of government, industry, academia and private nonprofit organizations interested in new and timely reports on the ecological pulse of the region. In a very real way, the Penobscot Bay Marine Resources Collaborative, which the Island Institute has administered for the past four years, served as a vital pilot program for GOMOOS. The collaborative has successfully demonstrated that the best way to understand complex marine resource issues in a place like Penobscot Bay or the Gulf of Maine is through a sustained program of integrated ocean observations. The complexity of the observations, which take advantage of new buoy and remote sensing technologies, fundamentally depends on marine organizations and fisheries associations pooling their talent and resources.

Another initiative launched last year has not yet landed in the promised land, but follows the model established by the Pen Bay Collaborative and GOMOOS. This effort, spearheaded by the Davis Conservation Foundation, has brought together a broad cross section of government, fishermen's associations, nonprofits and research institutions to seek federal support for ecosystem-based collaborative research. Our aim is at once simple and immense: to fund marine research to understand the marine biodiversity on which the future of the Gulf of Maine region depends.

What is exciting in many of these new Gulf of Maine initiatives is the growing recognition among fishermen, private nonprofits, the state university system and government that the old models of competing against each other for scarce resources does not work. The "old science" model in which a respected scientist responds to a request for proposals in a national competition is good for advancing some kinds of scientific endeavors. This model, however, is not good for building long-term, working partnerships that are built as much on personal relationships as on intellectual challenges. We are trying to develop a new model based on true collaboration, one that integrates marine users, including fishermen, into the process of setting priorities for the kinds of questions that need to be addressed. It will take truly far sighted scientists to feel comfortable enough to make room for others in thinking through challenges that were once the their prerogative alone.

At the Institute we are reshaping our roles to respond to the changing conditions and challenges that confront us at the different scales of our activity. We will continue to operate at multiple, linked scales throughout the islands and Gulf of Maine. We will continue to hone our skills as facilitators in collaborations, and we intend to expand the number of partnerships in which we are active. We will be rigorous in evaluating our existing projects. We will define the value-added dimensions we bring to our programs and partnerships. We will increase our efforts to raise funds for other groups and organizations that are in a better position to deliver services than we are. And we will continue to believe that a rising tide floats all boats.

"... like no other place I have ever lived"

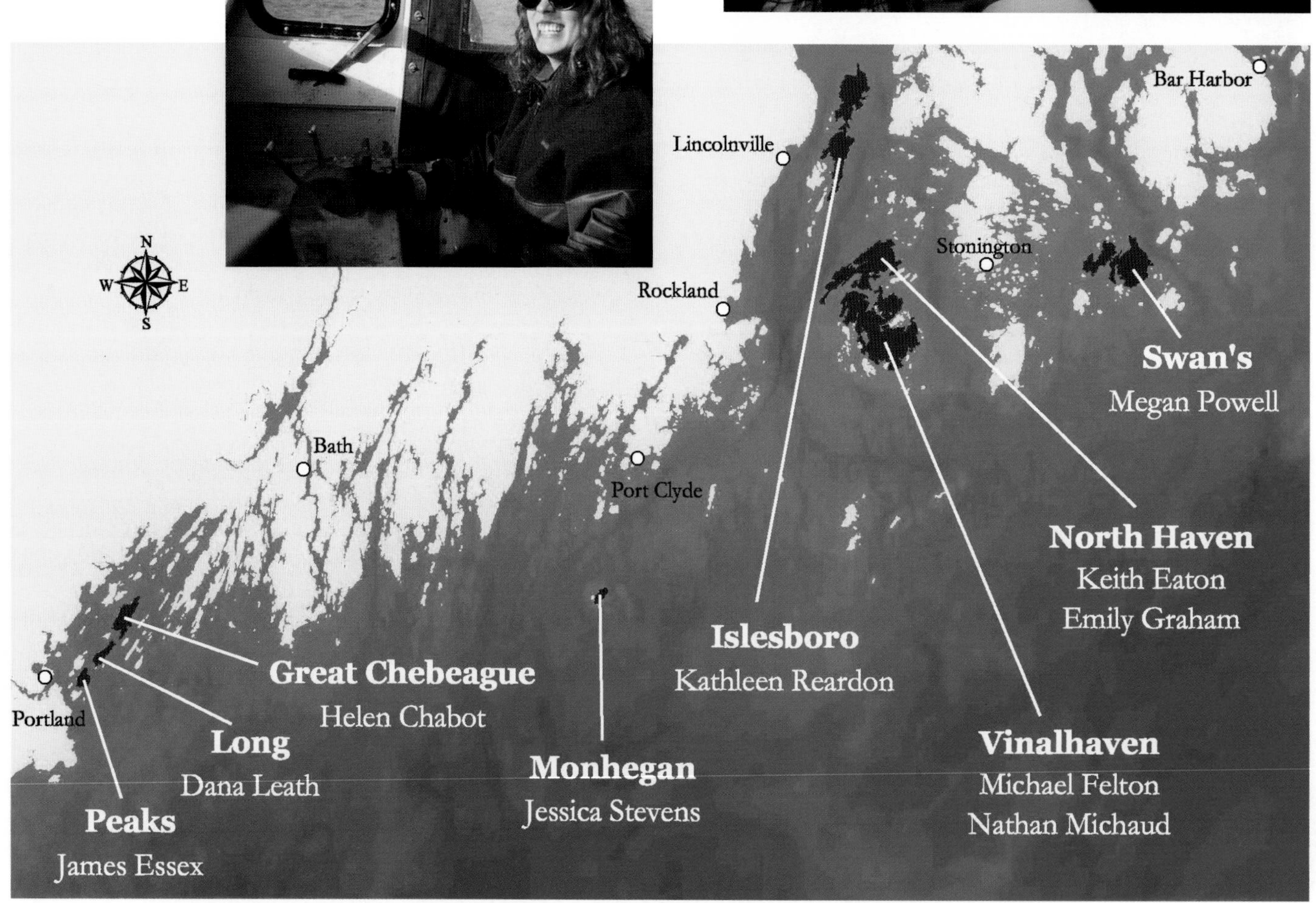

Andy Boyce

Island Fellows join the lives of eight communities

A new Island Institute program places recent college graduates as "fellows" at the invitation of island communities. This past winter ten Island Fellows lived on islands from Casco Bay to the Mt. Desert area. They functioned as teachers, sea-samplers, coaches, consultants, volunteers and participants in a variety of community projects. Most important, they did their best to become full-fledged members of their adopted communities. All have been encouraged to write about their experiences, and what follows is a sampling of thoughts from this season's group.

Helen Chabot, Fellow on Chebeague, and student helper Britny Bernier at the Chebeague Island school

HELEN CHABOT, CHEBEAGUE

Coming to terms with a mouse

OCT. 2, 2000:

... I have realized that part of living on an island is about depending on other people to give you a hand when you need it, and to return that favor when you get the chance. Unlike the mainland, where there are services around that you can pay to access, like 24-hour taxi service or roadside assistance, out here people call on their neighbor to help them out. Coming from my staunchly independent past, with my fear of inconveniencing other people by asking them for help, this may take some getting used to. But I think this is one of the great things of an island community, and one that I am happy to be a part of.

DEC. 1, 2000:

Somehow [measuring lobsters] seemed more glamorous in my imagination. The wind blowing the smells of the sea to my face, the waves glistening in the sun, the reassuring hum of the engine. In real life it was more like the stench of thawing bait, the choppy water rocking the boat threatening me with nausea, and the roar of the engine and winch that makes it hard to even hear myself think. No, it's not really that bad at all, but I must say it was a little different from what I expected.

DEC. 11, 2000:

Last night I had a showdown with a mouse. It wasn't a very big one, maybe two inches long, light brown with beady little eyes and whitish ears that twitched as it looked at me. You would think I wouldn't be intimidated by something so small and harmless looking. But the sad truth is, at this point of the battle at least, it's winning.

I didn't count on the speed and jumping ability of this little fellow. Every time I cleared away another box or container, it would scamper away and hide behind something else. I got to the other end of the shelf and found my friend hiding behind a bottle of vegetable oil. I grabbed the bottle with one hand and with the other tried to grab the mouse, but again I was too slow and the mouse took off for the other end of the cabinets... I decided to let the mouse be, contained in the cupboard, and go skate off some of my frustrations. The skating was great, the pond had just opened the day before, and lots of the kids from school were there. I was amazed at the setup: along one wall of the hut were boxes and boxes of ice skates, shelves of helmets, and buckets full of hockey sticks. "You can just help yourself to whatever equipment you need, and bring it back at the end of the season. Or leave any old skates you don't need anymore here for others to use," it was explained to me. What a great system.

But back to my mouse adventures. I proceeded to block off one end of the shelf with a notebook. I thought it was high enough to block any passage, but apparently the inch of space I'd left at the top was enough for the mouse to jump over, which it promptly did. Standing on my chair I could clearly see the mouse. I probably could have grabbed the mouse when I first saw it, but the longer we stared at each other the more nervous I got. It was a battle of nerves and it was winning...

Luckily for the mouse the island store had already closed for the day. I dreamt all night of mice and rats and of different ways of trying to catch them. In the morning I went to the store, where the folks provided me with a variety of interesting ways to catch mice, involving various combinations of buckets, pots, cheese and peanut butter. When I got back home and finally worked up the nerve to open the cabinet I didn't see the mouse at all.

I was inwardly relieved at not having to have another direct confrontation with the mouse, with each of us staring each other down, watching the other's every move. I set up a bucket and peanut butter contraption in the cabinet, as recommended by one of the folks in the store, and am still waiting for the results.

EMILY GRAHAM, NORTH HAVEN

The meaning of darkness in winter

Taking the ferry back to North Haven this evening was beautiful. Coming in to the island the water was like a mirror, completely still, reflecting the boats and the lights of the little downtown area. Before coming into the ferry landing and town, though, there were very few lights. I knew that there were houses all along the shore there; I wondered why. When one of the students came by, I asked him. No lights because the houses belong to summer people. The darkness was so striking to me — a real, physical manifestation of that sharp divide between those who are here year round and those who just come for the summer. It all sort of came together for me — a first real glimpse of understanding North Haven and the seasons of people who live here.

Winter has come to North Haven. I like the phrase that winter has come, it implies that winter is something that exists — something that visits for a while. It's true, and it's our turn to have winter as a guest for a while. It seems to be settling in, too: we got about 4 inches last night and this morning.

I am going to the mainland. I have an appointment that I could have canceled, but it is such a struggle to have to schedule mainland activities. I had better go when I have the chance. I long to have a winter day to stay on the island, to absorb the silence. Life is life, it's busy, sometimes hectic, always full, mostly lacking time to let the silence in. When I find it, though, it is unmistakable.

Emily Graham, North Haven Fellow, aboard a mussel raft with Joe Mariano of the Institute staff

I had a winter day today. School was canceled. A strong windstorm blew all yesterday, last night and this morning, knocking out power and collapsing trees over the roads. There was no snow but a snow day was called. It was a perfect day, those that I had anticipated having more of moving here. I sat and wrote all day long, letters and Christmas cards. I went for a walk. The days are so short that with school and meetings, I have very little free time in the daylight. I enjoyed having a full day of it today.

Mike Felton, Vinalhaven

A teacher teaches

One set of fraternal twins, one set of identical twin girls, amazing writers, gifted painters, an athlete who is already a junior legend in the high school and elementary school, a student whose comments drive Mom and teachers to fits of frustration and bouts of laughing, a boy who one week is present but really not there and the next is working diligently to complete his work, a girl who has a maturity and depth of thinking that might propel her to any of the nation's best universities or colleges. These are only a few of the personalities who combine to form the Vinalhaven 7th grade. It is our responsibility to form a class in which we work together so that we both might succeed; themselves as students and myself as a teacher.

History is more complete when we include more of the context, causes, and origin of events, movements and peoples. These events, movements and people are central parts of American History. To ignore them is to ignore the truth and to be blind to the whole story. Serious students of history need to see both the darkness and the possible light emerging from that darkness. To not recognize the darkness prevents one from being able to appreciate where the light emerged from, or the context from which the light shines. Moreover, students need to focus on the tragedies of American history so that they might address possible continuations of those tragedies in their nation's society today.

Vinalhaven is like no other place I have ever lived. Small population, lots of relatives, lobsters, lobster boats, lobster traps, lobster industry, lobster economy, lobster money, pickup trucks, kindness and openness among the people here, struggles to change, and possibility. The potential energy is vast, especially in the school around the students. There is much to be done. Change comes slow to Vinalhaven. But it comes.

Mrs. Merrill. She has taught me about personal pronouns, classroom management, France, art, and teaching. Humility, humor and skill are all strong characteristics of this teacher. She is good at what she does.

James Essex, Peaks Island

As the world turns

Here comes the day, another spin into the path of the Sun's rays. Today is a little different — ice coats the trees concentrating and refracting the light like a million different suns, a beautiful show. Ocean is calm. Atmosphere is calm. As suspected, the thermometer is broken, it shouldn't be 10 degrees F with the sun already turned on. I push on the door in a vain attempt to nudge the Earth's tilt back in a favorable orientation, and imagine stealing a few moments of summer from the people on the south half of the planet. A tough Maine raven, too proud to retreat south, breaks silence as it lifts from a tree perch, an unnoticed event without the ice but at present, the branch flexes and the ice cracks. The raven has cracked today's whip. Time to work, not outside today, the winter solstice, for no other reason than theoretically it should be the coldest of the year. I'm told a few less photons reach Peaks during this revolution through the Sun's rays than yesterday or tomorrow.

This day, like the previous 99 I've spent on Peaks, will be devoted to developing a working knowledge and record of the spatial and temporal distribution of matter and energy on Peaks Island. The mix of technology used to catalog and define where things are and when things happen entertain me into the night.

There goes the day, just like it started; calm ocean, calm atmosphere, broken thermometer.

Kathleen Reardon, Islesboro

Environmental science and an energy crisis

NOV. 3, 2000:

I hope that I get to do more with marine resources and systems, but presently Jon Kerr, the island teacher with whom I'm working, is very interested in the GIS aspect of my background (however small it may be). He told me about calling someone from the fire department whom he had been talking to about me, and who is interested in learning how he might be able to map the ponds of the island. And he also mentioned the groundwater commission. And the clam flats. Then the class came in.

Later in the afternoon, I went out with the AP Environmental Science class to walk down a mini-watershed. It was very interesting to see the students out in the field... When we finally arrived at the head of the salt marsh, Jon warned all of us to be wary of the sinkholes and random creeks where you could all of a sudden be up to your waist in water. We found an area that had three skeletons of deer

Kathleen Reardon examines a GIS project with Laura McCarthy at the Vinalhaven school.

remains. We assumed that the deer died because of falling into the stream as they were all either in the stream or immediately adjacent. It was an unsettling sight.

NOV. 19, 2000:
A quiet day, but I did have a neat experience. Yeah, I've seen deer around the house — usually running away — but today I was walking around the woods and as I came out into a clearing, I noticed a deer about 30 feet away, eating. It was eating grass and for about five minutes seemed completely oblivious of my presence. For a while, I stood next to the tree at the edge of the clearing. The deer looked up at me at one point, but didn't seem to see me. Then I moved slowly (and as silently as I could) to a rock to sit and watch. Each crunch of my feet on the leaves made me think it would run away. It didn't until I stepped on a big bunch of leaves. The deer jumped a little and looked around. I think she saw me, but she went back to eating looking up every minute or so - straight at me. I must have sat there watching a deer eat for 20 or 30 minutes. Beautiful!

DEC. 18, 2000:
Here I am writing by candlelight. It wasn't snow, but it was one incredible storm. From the rain that started just as I came home Saturday night till mid-afternoon today (Monday) when the cold front finally cleared things out — the weather has been insane. It poured all Saturday night, raining in sheets that pounded against my windows. And with that rain came wind, lots of it. The weather reports said normal gusts of 35 to 40 with some extreme gusts of 50 to 60. All day Sunday the winds blew. Every once in a while the power would flicker, but it didn't go out. Mid-Sunday, I drove down to the Town Beach at the southern end of the island to see what the water was doing. Although nothing like it probably was off Vinalhaven or Isle au Haut (what I would have given to see that!), the waves seemed as if they were eating the shore. The power of the wind and waves was amazing.

Now it is Monday. My power didn't go out until early this morning. I woke up around 6 a.m. to a branch beating continually against one of the skylights, and to darkness. My power had died. Fortunately, when the sun came out later today, it heated the house so I didn't have to worry about the pipes while I went in to the school. At school, everything was controlled chaos with all the little kids outside and the older students upstairs in study halls. Without power, the school had no water or, more importantly, bathrooms or lunch capabilities so the kids went home by noon.

It is dark and it is only 5 in the evening. Luckily I do have some candles and water jugs put aside, as well as a wood stove. I'm very thankful that I was able to find a house with a wood stove or I'd be out of luck right now. But this wood stove isn't the most efficient hunk of metal and I'll be getting up every few hours through the night to add more wood to prevent me and my pipes from freezing. It is all an adventure...

KEITH EATON, NORTH HAVEN

Where do I live?

JAN. 1, 2001:
Below gauzy clouds illuminated by the moon, in a crowd waiting for a lift to the basketball game, I faltered in my explanation of where it is I live. Asa was curious. I mentioned the location of the house and the color, the style of clapboard finish. "Macie W–'s house," Nancy chimed in over my shoulder. I should have known better than to try and describe a property's characteristics when there was shorthand available. Properties are not referred to by physique or street number, but, instead, are referred to by current owner, previous owner, or original owner, sometimes dating back to the Revolution. The Curtis farm. Waterman's farm. Cooper's. Ames'. Directions often come through this code as well, assuming I know. "Two driveways past the South Shore Brown's, before Greenway's." (This scenario is hypothetical.)

Generally, if I sit tight, knowing full well that the import of a conversation has been lost on me, the depth of understanding will come in time. Besides, I wouldn't want to be "known," or typed through the course of one conversation. Like the Hunter lyric says, "beneath the cool, calm face of the sea, / swift undertow."

Learning, the lifelong process. D was telling me about an idea he'd had for applied science and math once, an idea that came to fruition. He and the students at North Haven Community School had looked into the possibility of building a boat. They settled on a rowing gig. It sounded to me like a complicated process as it involved grants, sketched plans, new tools, etc. They even erected a shed in which to build the boat. I remember asking D, one day, if he'd ever built anything bigger than a canoe. He looked straight at me and calmly said, "No." I understood it immediately. Well, almost.

You want something done? When it comes to the Internet, sure, I can navigate it, know plenty of websites and the theoretical aspects of hypertext and what not, but I've never learned html, or the basics of site design even. Neither has Ian, my student. We want to build a site to describe the school's recently completed boat, RECOVERY, and we'll learn as we go along. Claris Home Page isn't that different than word-processing and Ian is jumping far ahead of me, impatient as I follow every step of the tutorial. In his mind, he's five steps ahead, uploading image files of the boat and prepping an MPEG video for online viewing. I want to make sure that we know the tool bar first.

But this is it, education going both ways, student teaching teacher teaching student, in an environment where if you can't accomplish a task for yourself, or can't find someone with whom to collaborate, it most likely will not get done. Besides, chances are that anything you want to accomplish isn't that difficult. People design these things, thus people can figure them out. When my car wasn't starting, D helped me isolate the problem, taking apart the dashboard and removing a squirrel's nest of wires surrounding a jerry-rigged alarm system. Normally, I wouldn't have dared. In lieu of a tow onto the ferry for an "expert" mainland opinion, our trouble-shooting made sense, and my, didn't she handle nicely in the snow today!

Dana Leath and Long Island school students during winter physical education class

Dana Leath, Long Island

Every day I learn something new

JAN. 4, 2001:

Exactly a month ago, on December 4, 2000, I loaded my belongings into my car and drove north, from Falls Church, Virginia, to Rockland, Maine. The following day, I reported in at the Island Institute excited to begin my next Maine experience, living and working in a remote island community. After a couple weeks of training and orientation in Rockland, I moved out to Long Island and began my placement as an Island Institute Fellow.

Long Island is located about four and half miles off Portland, in Casco Bay. Neighboring islands include Peaks Island, Chebeague Island and Cliff Island. Long Island is approximately three miles long and less than a mile wide. About 200 people are year-round residents of the island. Every day, I learn something new about the islanders, the island and the community's history.

I work at the 16-student, two-classroom, K-5 Long Island School. While the regular teacher is out on maternity leave, I am teaching the physical education class twice a week. In addition, I help with reading, math, writing, recess and other school activities as needed. I enjoy being back in elementary school and it is interesting to see how small island schools operate.

I am hoping to organize some activities and outings for the middle and high school students on the island. They attend school in Portland and there is not much for them to do here on the island. For a while now, the community has wanted to come up with something for the island teenagers to do, but no one has had the time or energy to do anything yet. Human resources are often a limiting factor in a small island community.

The other major component of my fellowship position is sea sampling — measuring and recording data about lobsters. The data is used by the Island Institute and the Maine Department of Marine Resources to help understand and assess the lobster fishery. This is valuable information because lobsters are a critical component to the economic vitality of most island communities. After I complete sea sampling training, I'll go out on a lobster boat from Long Island once a week and collect data.

With time, once I know the community better and people here are more familiar with me, I will be able to get involved with the community in other ways. I think the biggest challenge will be trying to start a program or make a difference in a way that is self-sustaining and will continue on after my fellowship position is over.

I like it here on Long Island. It's quiet and peaceful and life is slower and simpler. There is time each day to enjoy simple things like the sunrise, the silence, the ocean, the snow-frosted trees, the individual qualities of the children at the school, and the pleasure of stopping by the post office to talk with the postmaster and check my P.O. box.

Nate Michaud, Vinalhaven

Witnessing an island's planning process

JANUARY 2, 2001:

The beginning of this placement is certainly different from the last. The last one started in June, when Vinalhaven was just starting its summer hum. The island has its winter walls up now. In June I got here in a rush; because I was late in applying, the details of my fellowship were worked out at the last minute. But I've been looking forward to — and, with Sandy Thomas and Stefan Pukulski at the Island Institute, planning for — this placement since I left for Virginia in August.

In June I knew that I only had two hectic months to collect oral history and record lobster catches. I'm now signed up for eight months (I look forward to seeing winter dissolve into spring and spring into summer here). And in June the fellowship program was still in its infancy — I was one of two fellows. A semester later and I'm one of ten. Sandy's certainly got her hands full now.

Those whom I've talked to about the fellowship program on Vinalhaven seem happy with it. Mike, who's been working in the school since I left, is getting along great with the kids (no surprise there, given his great attitude and energy). And I've heard no complaints about the work I did last summer. The lobstermen I went sea-sampling with all said they'd be interested in continuing the project when the season comes back around, and Roy and Esther at the historical society seem pleased with the oral histories; they also want to continue that work this winter. I learned a lot doing both things, and I'm confident that I'll be able to do a better job at both of them this time around.

Of course the main work will be the comprehensive planning process, which I'm a little anxious about, since I'll be learning as I go. But I'm also excited — a community deciding what it is and what it wants to be is interesting stuff. It also fits in well with my interest in tourism (I actually hope to focus the remainder of my Ph.D. work on these areas when I return to William & Mary). I think witnessing Vinalhaven's planning process and helping out however I can will be an invaluable experience. As I've heard others say, the process of creating a comprehensive plan is at least as important as the finished plan itself.

Megan Powell, Swan's Island

A diversity of folks, sharing the wonders of a single island

Riding on the ferry for 30 minutes, the hot sun that had warmed me all afternoon couldn't compete with the wind and I was soon reaching for my sweatshirt. Although goose bumps had begun to appear on my arms I wouldn't budge from my outside seat on the upper deck. The sight of the water and sky, blue on blue, was too much to allow a compromise of the view. The first-time ride behind a sheet of glass in the cabin wouldn't have satisfied my curiosities.

The boat's engine hummed loudly, but the constant sound almost floated away as my other senses opened to the surroundings. The air smelled like the cold ocean water, reminding me of how long it had been since I visited the sea. Little buoys of bright colors waved, dotting the otherwise uninterrupted blue. Knowing almost nothing of the lobster business, I correctly imagined that these marked the traps.

I glanced down at the cars — their plates, like the buoys, were different colors — signifying different home states of the owners. Must be warm enough to have people vacationing from the more southern regions, I thought. A diversity of folks were sharing the wonders of a single island. Children were bouncing about, talking between giggles as they investigated the ferry and the sea below from every angle.

The island was within my view and I looked back, momentarily intent on determining from what nook in the horizon we had emerged. Now the mainland seemed like a chain of islands in the distance with the majestic mountains of Acadia pushing towards the sky. I turned forward, toward my new home for the next year. The evergreens crowded the shoreline, waving in the wind to greet us. The island appeared to be a miniature world of its own.

Island Fellows, left to right: Kathleen Reardon, Megan Powell, James Essex, Helen Chabot, Nathan Michaud, Dana Leath, Mike Felton, Jessica Stevens, Emily Graham, Keith Eaton

JESSICA STEVENS, MONHEGAN

So much to learn

MARCH 14, 2001

Sea sampling. A whole new set of lobstermen and boats to get to know. Out on the PANDORA today, a big boat. Plenty of room to dance! Measured a few lobsters. We hauled some shrimp traps. All new to me. Small mesh and a small entrance. Had shrimp for dinner. Go-od!

APRIL 3, 2000

I taught my first lesson at school today. About sea sampling, lobster tagging, why I had moved to Monhegan. It was difficult planning the lesson; teaching it was even harder. It's been a long time since I've been around kids regularly. Wasn't sure at what level to explain what I was doing. Basically we unpacked my sea sampling box, discussing what each item in the box was used for. And I had the kids come up with questions about my job and about lobsters that we'll try to answer during the spring. They were interested. Amazing how much they did not know about lobsters. Then again, before I began doing lobster research a year ago, I didn't know much about lobsters or lobstering either...

MAY 20, 2000

Finished tagging lobsters today! Ended with tag #998. Taking into account the tags that broke I think that the fishermen and I tagged over 900 short lobsters. There's still 2,000 new tags sitting in my fish tote, but logistics were against us. Everyone is starting to pull their traps from the tagging area and the season closes on the 29th so I don't think I'll get more than a few regular sea sampling trip in from here on out.

SEPT. 14, 2000

On the computer nearly the entire day analyzing data. One of those perfect September days, sun streaming and cool, when it is hard to concentrate on work. Fortunately, I have a great office...only a big picture window stood between me and the Harbor. Fun to glance up and watch the goings-on every so often as I organized rows and columns of information about tagged lobsters. Calm. Southwest breeze.

The tag data is looking interesting. About 30 lobsters have been recaptured since May. Some are just over the Monhegan line or a little further north. But some are moving further than I expected.

DEC. 6, 2000

Met with Tralice today about the progress I'm making on the Museum's marine exhibit. My grant proposal to the Maine Community Foundation was accepted! No more just dreaming that I'll get to go scuba diving.... We want to show that the topography underwater is just as dramatic as the Monhegan that's above water... I hope we can pull this off.

DEC. 20, 2000:

Katlin and the school kids are coming over today to make cookies for the upcoming school play.

At 9 a.m., the expected knock on the door, followed by a blur of bodies shedding coats and mittens and six pairs of boots that ended up on the floor in varying degrees of orderliness.

Out came the ragged, splattered, hand-copied recipe. Then, we were juggling ingredients, bowls, measuring spoons, instructions, and students to produce a cooperative math lesson. Wolfie scooped brown sugar. Claire measured salt. Stirring jobs were shared to keep arms from tiring. Mounds of dough were arranged and rearranged until they formed square-number patterns that fit the cookie sheets to Kyle and Marisa's satisfaction. Then, into the oven went the sheets and minutes began to be counted....

Soon, not only had we produced three batches of my favorite oatmeal-raisin cookies packed up in wax paper and Tupperware, but all the dishes were clean again and everyone was happy with the amount of crumb-testing in which they participated. Last but not least, as with all my recipes, a quick comment was agreed upon and composed on back of the crumpled page: "12/12/00, made with the fabulous schoolchildren and the fabulous teacher, best when eaten warm."

Since this article was written an additional Fellow, Erin Fisher, has taken up residence on Deer Isle to work with the Stonington Fisheries Alliance.

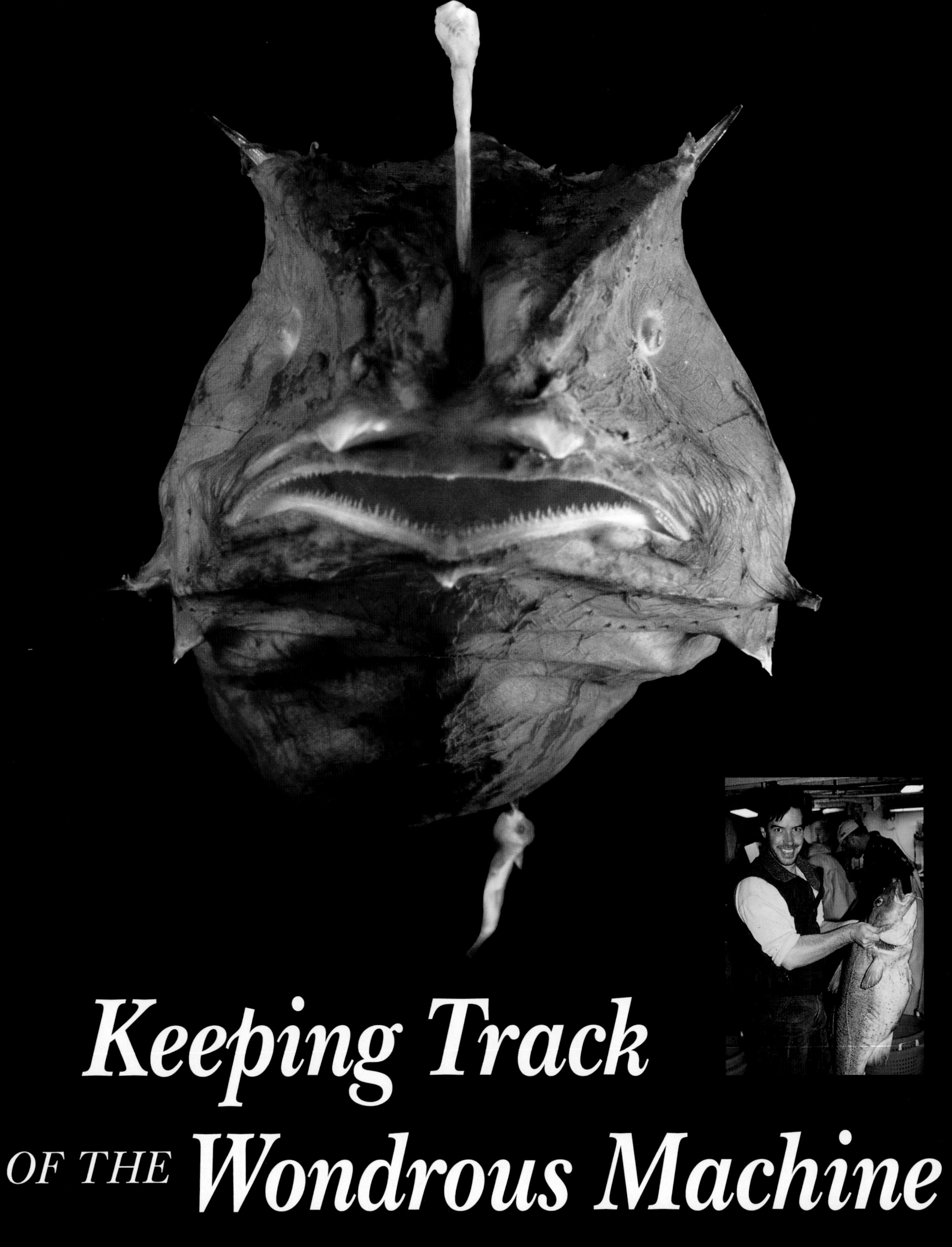

Keeping Track OF THE *Wondrous Machine*

BENJAMIN NEAL

To know what's out there in the Gulf of Maine, we've got to measure it (literally)

Bill Curtsinger

Midnight. With a high cirrus deepening and thickening into layers, it will soon be a night without stars. The wind is only perhaps 15 knots, just having shifted to the southeast, but an intermittent high keening sound in the rigging hints that something stronger is on the way. The crescent moon appears sporadically, wreathed in fleeing clouds, and then is extinguished from sight. It is the next-to-last day on the last leg of the autumn National Marine Fisheries Service groundfish trawl survey. My watch is just turning out for our six hours on deck.

The Fisheries Service has the difficult and often contentious task of managing and conserving the United States' valuable marine fish stocks. Providing an effective management strategy means having an understanding of the underlying physical and biological processes that control the abundance of these species, and to this end the Service conducts various annual at-sea surveys. Last October I was invited to participate as a guest member of the scientific staff.

The purpose of this trip was to assess the regional abundance of the Gulf of Maine's groundfish stocks. Estimates made from data collected on this and other similar trips will have a direct influence on management practices as they are used in the development of the yearly catch quotas, the length of season and determining open areas for fishing.

This survey, which dates back to 1885, is the longest running fish assessment of its kind, and is universally recognized as one of the most scientifically valuable time series in the world.

The surveys are done on vessels operated by the National Oceanographic and Atmospheric Administration (NOAA). I was aboard the venerable ALBATROSS IV, built for this work in 1962, and which continues to this day to be the primary vessel for the trawl surveys. She is 187 feet in length and is equipped with stern trawl fishing gear, as well as plankton collecting equipment, processing tables, large freezers and a lab for preserving samples. The ship also provides accommodations and support for the 32 scientists, officers, crew and fishermen who work on board. Shipboard life is a routine of six hours on, six hours off. I work from midnight to just after dawn, have breakfast, then wake just before lunch and work until dinner. Obviously meals take on a special importance in this schedule, certainly as events to look forward to, but after a week they also serve to remind one of what time of the day it really is.

Left (inset): The author

SCALES, OTOLITHS AND STOMACHS

These standard groundfish trawl surveys are conducted twice annually, in the spring and the fall. Each survey consists of four legs, and each leg may have as many as 75 individual stations, each consisting of a 30-minute tow of the net at a prescribed speed (3.85 knots), with the entire catch coming on deck for sorting, identification and dissection by the scientific crew. The sex and maturity of fish are noted, and scales, otoliths (small bones in the heads of fishes, used for determining ages of individuals) and stomachs (for determining feeding ecology) are collected. Whole fish also may be collected and frozen for later shoreside use.

ALBATROSS IV

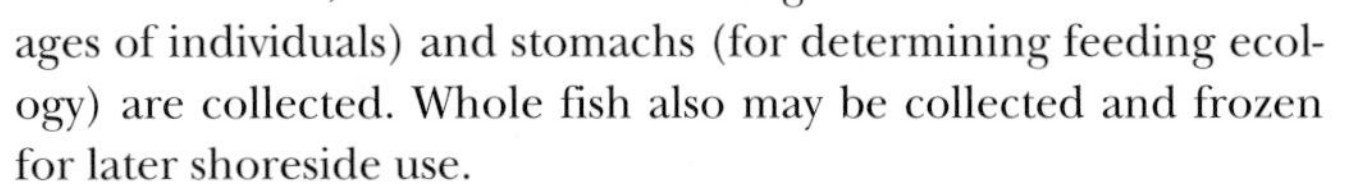

Sampling requirements are dictated by individual requests; on my cruise there were 33 separate requests, mostly from fisheries service scientists, but also from universities and research groups as far afield as Great Britain and Wisconsin. CTD (Conductivity, Temperature and Depth) measuring equipment is lowered at each station, and at selected stations a twin plankton net also is towed to assess primary productivity. In this way the ecosystem is measured from the lowest level of the food chain.

In my kitbag I carry an invaluable reference work, *Fishes of the Gulf of Maine,* by Henry Bigelow and William Schroeder, commonly referred to as "Bigelow and Schroeder." Published in 1953, this 577-page volume is still considered an authority on topics such as the range of species, their breeding habits, abundance and physical description. The book is noted for its accurate documentation of historical sightings (going as far back as John Smith's *Generall Historie of Virginia, New England and the Summer Isles,* 1616), its evocative and expressive line illustrations and vivid prose (at least to those interested in fishes), and I keep my old copy handy-by on deck for any questions I might have.

The Gulf of Maine is described somewhat loosely by Bigelow and Schroeder as "the oceanic bight from Nantucket Shoals and Cape Cod on the west, to Cape Sable on the east, thus it includes the shore lines of northern Massachusetts, Maine, and parts of New Brunswick and of Nova Scotia." The National Marine Fisheries Service, for the purpose of its survey work, takes a more limited definition, and does not include Georges Bank or Canadian waters in the scope of our trip. (Georges Bank is covered by another leg dedicated especially to that rich and vast area, and the Canadians do the same for their waters.)

The Gulf of Maine by any definition can be described as a semi-enclosed body of water, with a complex bathymetry of banks, swells, ledges and deep water basins. First noted on 16th century French charts as the "Sea of Norumbega," these waters contain some of the most prolific fishing grounds in the world, grounds that have stood nearly four centuries of intensive fishing for cod, haddock, hake, flounders, halibut, redfish and other finfish, as well as crustaceans and shellfish. Cape Cod, Browns Bank, Jeffreys Ledge, Stellwagen Bank and Cashes Ledge are all well known to generations of New England fishermen, and it is in this fruitful and storied region that we make our sampling tows.

We depart from Cape Cod, ranging east towards the Hague Line separating Canadian and American waters, then north to the Maine coast, and finally west and south to Cape Cod Bay, returning to Woods Hole through the Cape Cod Canal.

There are over 200 species of fish and shellfish native to these waters, of which only 40 or 50 are harvested commercially. We generally catch only the demersal, or bottom dwelling, inhabitants. We do bring up some quantity of the vast shoals of herring and mackerel that serve as fodder fish for much of the rest of the ecosystem, but we do not encounter any of the larger, highly migratory predators roaming the Gulf. The giant bluefin, the world's fastest and most valuable fish, is a yearly summer visitor to the Gulf, arriving when the water temperature is above 50 degrees and schools of herring and mackerel make the living easy. Bigelow and Schroeder credit a 1,225-pounder brought into Boston in 1913 as the official record, but hint at rumors of 1,600-pounders. Bluefin of any size are rare in autumn; globetrotting adventurers that they are, these powerful fish potentially could be wandering among the West Indies, sliding through Gibraltar into the warmth of the Mediterranean or basking in the sunny Azores. Quarter-ton swordfish and ten-foot great white sharks also could be circling beneath us in the water column, but these "apex" fish are not our quarry.

Our interest is the smaller fishes of the bottom, the numerous and productive species that make up most of the biomass, like the blades of grass that sustain the terrestrial world. It is a good thing that we are not looking for the giants, for they are more elusive now than they ever were, as their tribes regretfully have been reduced to only fractions of what they once were.

One of the more commonly seen fish on our trip is, of course, the famous and depleted Atlantic cod. We generally catch a basket or so of codfish on most hauls, for perhaps a total of 50 pounds, mainly scrod and medium fish. There are a few individuals this night weighing up to about 15 pounds, but the average is probably well under five. We measure and dissect the fish, noting sex and reproductive state. We check their stomachs for their contents, remove their otoliths for further aging study back in the lab, and return the rest to the sea.

Cod were the fish that brought the first distant water fishermen and European settlers to the shores of the new world. Around the first millennium, Viking voyages, probably not coincidentally, covered much of the range of the Atlantic cod. Well before Columbus, Basque fishermen were marketing large quantities of salt cod in medieval markets, keeping silent on the location of their fishing grounds. After 1500, waves of English, Dutch, Portuguese and French immigrants to the New World began pulling boatloads of codfish from the sea. The easily preserved, low-fat cod continued to be the mainstay of the commercial fisheries in the Gulf of Maine until ice became plentiful in the mid-19th century, when fresh haddock was subsequently welcomed in the markets.

Sometime in the darkest hours of the night, with the bright sodium lights and the fishing routine focusing the consciousness down to little else than the patch of wet steel on which we would dump the next haul, from the net spills out the largest cod I have ever seen. Fifty-one pounds and almost four feet long, with

After a 30-minute tow, the entire catch comes on deck.

stocky shoulders on a swelling olive-green back speckled with striking yellow spots, and a snowy white belly, this fish seems too large and heavy out of the water to flop about like its smaller brethren. She (large fish of this size are surely females, a fact we later confirm by examining this fish) lies quite still, with the placidity that seems to be common to the largest individuals of any species. The size of her head brings to mind the various cod-head recipes I have seen in older cookbooks ("take one large Cod heade . . ."), and makes me understand how such a head truly could be expected to provide sustenance for a whole family. I reach down and lift her with both arms, close to her deep amber eyes, larger than my own. We put the mighty fish in a basket of its own, and put her on the scale.

After the haul I pull out my battered Bigelow and Schroeder and found out that this fish is likely at least ten years old, and that while she is the queen of this particular trip, she is far from being a record for her kind. While most cod are caught when they are under ten or 12 pounds, the species can attain tremendous sizes. The largest on record dates from May 1895, when a longliner off the Massachusetts coast brought up a six-foot giant weighing 211-and-a-quarter pounds; another is noted as tipping the scales at 138 pounds dressed (it must have been over 180 pounds live) caught by a handliner on Georges Bank in 1838. Another of 100 pounds is recorded from Wood Island in Saco Bay, taken April 9, 1883, and noted as having a 17-and-a-half inch head. The largest "recent" reference in the book dates from early July 1922, when a 90-pounder was taken in Maine coastal waters. However, then as now, any fish over 70 pounds is exceptional, and large fish are considered to be any over about 20 pounds. Our fish that night elicits such admiration even from the seasoned fishermen that she is not sent back to the sea, but rather split and cleaned for salting by one of the Portuguese fishermen in the time-honored fashion.

The common codfish is quite uncommon in its incredible fecundity. It has been said that if all the eggs of spawning cod survived to maturity, they would displace all the water from the Gulf of Maine within three years. Bigelow and Schroeder notes a 52-and-one-half inch fish, roughly equivalent to the fish we took that night, that yielded 8,989,094 eggs. A more common three-foot fish could produce three million, and an average ten-pounder at least a million.

Unfortunately, this productivity was still not enough to keep the population of cod ahead of human fishing pressure. Decades of intense fishing by modern fishing trawlers have caused a drastic decline in groundfish abundance, a decline that may or may not have yet reached rock bottom. This decline has led some observers to question whether or not some stocks can ever recover. I take it as perhaps a good sign that most of the cod we see are juveniles, waiting to rebuild the population if they are able to breed before they are caught.

EQUAL OPPORTUNITY PREDATORS AND THEIR FRIENDS

Not all of the fish that appear out of the net during these midnight hours are so photogenic and pleasant as the cod. One haul brings to our sorting table the writhing hagfish, by all appearances a worm of the bottom, grayish in color, scaleless, about a foot and a half long, without eyes or jaws or even true fins. This cartilaginous fish lives in the mud, scavenging whatever carrion drops from above. They are reviled by fishermen for eating their way into hooked or netted fishes, boring into the body cavities and eating out the intestines and the meat, leaving nothing but an empty sack of skin and bones. Their preference for the valuable haddock does nothing to improve their status. They complete their unpopularity by being prodigious producers of loathsome slime. Mucus sacs on either side of the abdomen can pour out this slime in quantities out of all proportion to the fish's small size, and Bigelow and Schroeder note that they do not consider reports of one hag filling a two-gallon bucket with slime to be an exaggeration. Luckily we catch few, and they seem well behaved, although not at all pleased to have been brought to a cold and windy deck in the middle of the night.

National Maine Fisheries Service (3)

The scientific crew sorts and identifies the catch.

Another common sight on the sorting table are the toothy, gaping jaws of the monkfish. This creature is officially called the American Goosefish, but is also known as monkfish, angler, poor-man's lobster, molligut, all-mouth, the fishing frog. Out of the water his soft body collapses, and somewhat resembles the flattened skate. The huge head and mouth make confusion with any other species unlikely, however. Almost half his body is head, and his mouth, which he insists on holding wide open, stretches the full width of his body. The rest of the body tapers off to the tail, where the only edible portion of the fish is to be found. This tremendous mouth serves to support the monkfish's vast and storied appetite. We examine the stomachs of those we catch and find all manner of finfish, some almost as long as the specimens we are examining. I read up later on the fish and am surprised to find a vast recorded diet, listing documented examples of just about every common species of fish having been found in the stomachs of this equal-opportunity predator as well as accounts of finding snails, grebes, ducks, loons, herring gulls, lobsters, sand dollars, sea turtles, hermit crabs and even eelgrass in their stomachs. Bigelow and Schroeder cite one particularly full monkfish as containing "21 flounders and a dogfish, all of marketable size."

Late in the night we take a small alligatorfish, an odd little fish armored with bony plates. This rigid covering gives him the odd industrial form of having an octagonal trunk tapering midway to hexagonal. A source in Bigelow and Schroeder describes him as "not much thicker or softer than an iron nail." I find him as we clean out the sorting box, his three-inch sticklike body hiding under a much larger pollock. Regardless of size, all creatures are measured, weighed and recorded, and thus I duly place him on the dissection table safely out of the wind that could blow him away.

My shift ends at six o'clock, and the second shift of scientists, whom I only see at these moments, arrive on deck. The wind has strengthened through the night to over 30 knots out of the southwest, and it finds damp and cold pathways to the skin at the neck and cuffs. Seas have built and salt spray mixes with a sharp blown rain; we slide buckets of fish across the wet deck, rather than trying to lift and walk with them. I welcome the thought of the warmth of my berth.

DREAM OF THE DEEP

I turn in just as the early gray light begins to show the shadows of bulky, white-horse combers rolling out to the horizon. There is no breaking dawn under the weighty sky, but only the diffuse spreading of a weak light. The view from my porthole runs from dim gray to black for seconds at a time as dark water reaches up and holds onto the side of the boat, as if reluctant to let go, but then does so as the vessel goes into the next deep roll. I wash my face free of salt, remove a few stray scales and climb into the bunk. I open my Bigelow and Schroeder and read for a bit on some of the rarer creatures we are sailing over. As the new day comes slowly to our patch of wind-rent gray water, I drift off into my own dark night of slumber, with the wild fishes of the Gulf of Maine swimming freely through my sea of dreams.

The occasional streaks of phosphorescence sparkling in the foam rushing past the porthole seem to become brighter in the blacked-out cabin. I watch them idly for a bit, and with the oncoming weight of sleep am transported down into the cold and deep, into the silent basins and black canyons of the shelves on the outer edge of the Gulf, where the flashes in the darkness become the firing of the illumination organs of deepwater fishes. In the unimaginable cold and pressure of depth I swim amongst the small-sized, large-eyed, and bizarrely bony inhabitants of one of the most inhospitable environments on earth. I glide past a viperfish, unmistakable with its skeleton-like head and underslung bulldog jaw. This thin, tapering fish grows only to about one foot, with several rows of small yellow-green luminescent spots running from throat to tail, flashing in the darkness like a miniature set of runway lights. A bizarre hatchetfish passes by, decorated with 96 light emitting organs in his three-inch length. That this thin fish's element is the very bottom of the sea is revealed by his eyes, which are fixed gazing upwards. I drift past the aptly named headlight fish, his entire snout covered with a large luminescent patch running from the jaw to the top of the head, and completely filling the space between the eyes. He flashes his light once and darts off into the darkness.

Bill Curtsinger (2)

Ocean Pout

As I descend into deeper sleep, my dreams seem to rise in the water column, and as I swim up onto the banks I surprise a halibut in his patient rest on the bottom. These famously large flat fishes grew rare in the Gulf early in the history of New World, one of the first species to show the effects of hard fishing. The market developed only about 1825, but by 1850 the inshore fishery was depleted to the point that few boats pursued them. Exceeded in size in the Gulf only by tuna, swordfish and some sharks, halibut begin their lives as tiny one-eighth inch diameter eggs, drifting free in the water column. According to Bigelow and Schroeder they once commonly grew to over 100 pounds, with the record being a 700-pounder caught off Cape Ann in 1917. Sadly they are rare in any quantity or size today.

As the line between self and fish becomes even more blurred in my imaginings, I encounter the rare deep-sea anglerfish. This deep water fish has a flattened body like the monkfish, and the same large mouth. Strikingly, however, this fish has developed a luminescent organ out at the end of a very long and slender tentacle, which protrudes out from its forehead and dangles in front of its mouth. This is the lure for prey, and slyly it can be drawn back by retractor muscles, pulling the ganglia rearward towards the head, bringing the bait (and the presumably unsuspecting prey) closer to the gaping maw. As I settle in and get to know this reclusive fish, I come to uncover the strange story of its marital arrangements. I consider my own relationships as I look upon the male, who reaches a size only about one-fifth that of the female. Males survive only by finding a female to attach to, boring a hole in her skin and growing right in place. Males have no teeth, no lure to attract food, no eyes, no alimentary canal, living off the very blood supply of the female. In fact, they are really little more than overgrown parasitic testicles. A large female can support more than one male, and there are records of fish being caught showing scars from broken-off past relationships. A three-footer of this species is recorded in Bigelow and Schroeder, weighing 20 pounds, with two males attached. This benthic fish found terrestrial fame for a day June 29, 1963, when it appeared in both the *Boston Globe* and the *Boston Post.* As the vessel rolls on, the work continuing above me on deck, my dreams of fishes fade and finally I sleep the sleep of the depths.

I awake, thick-headed and bleary-eyed, with five pounds of Bigelow and Schroeder lying on my chest, to the sight of translucent jade-green water reaching occasionally up to the level of my thick glass porthole, set about three feet above the waterline. My dreams of rare and ephemeral fishes are replaced by the anticipation of buckets of real ones. Sunlight glints from the wind-fractured surface of the sea, and I squint up at my watch, rolling from the reading light a foot above my bunk. The boat seems to be moving a bit less than it had when I turned in, although it is hard to tell from where I am. Almost high noon. Time to return to work. Even though it is midday I make my way to the deck by way of the coffee pot. The fresh breeze, the dancing seas and the certainty of fish waiting to be examined soon chase away any lingering slumber, and my watch heads back to work.

I arrive on the afterdeck just as the net is being hauled clear. The westerly wind is still around 20 knots, but it has that indefinable quality of weakening and decay, and the shredded cloud cover is rapidly evaporating into a smooth blue. The power of the night before is slipping away, and it leaves us all feeling refreshed and invigorated. An overflowing load of redfish is dumped on the table, and it is with a brisk lightness and cheer that fish begin flying through the air into the appropriate baskets

Redfish

Andrew J. Martinez

Scallop

The sweet redfish is sold as ocean perch, and is taking on an increasing importance in commercial catches. True to their name, they are a flaming orange-red color, and are found in a broad range throughout the region almost anywhere deeper than about 20 fathoms. These fish do not reach a large size, with a good-sized one being any over about a foot long. They are remarkably long lived. A ten-inch fish, just becoming sexually mature, is perhaps ten years old, and the larger individuals will be upwards of 20. It is quite likely that some of the redfish we see on the table are older than myself. This slow-growing trait has made them vulnerable to depletion by overfishing, and while redfish catches are increasing of late, harvests of this slowly-maturing fish must be carefully managed. Carefully labeled otoliths taken from all sizes will be examined onshore in the lab to draw up an age structure of the population.

As shadows flatten on the deck, so do the seas. The light northwest wind now brings a dry air, clean as the blue-green water, and the horizon shows sharp in unlimited visibility. The routine of sorting, cutting and recording continues in the warmth of the late afternoon sun, and in haul after haul we catalog the colorful diversity of the seafloor. Bathypolypus octopus that could fit in a shot glass, rubbery illex squid a foot long, knobby purple sea cucumbers, plate-sized scallops with their delicate fringe of eyes, gangly fragile spider crabs — all come across the sorting table. Stomach examinations reveal yet another complex layer of life, a lower trophic community of even smaller prey creatures — mysid, euphasiid and decapod shrimp, crunchy brittle stars, tunicates (sea squirts), ctenophores (comb jellies), tunicate worms and others.

Unnoticed in the work, the clock ticks around, and suddenly, fresh from dinner, in oilskins and boots, the other watch appears a few minutes early. The lower arm of the sun is just touching the edge of the horizon, and a glance to the east shows the spreading blue-black ink of oncoming night. The residual seas are long and oily-smooth in the evening calm, blending to a low red in a braided line that pulls us towards the setting sun. Day slopes into night once again over the Gulf of Maine and, while our boat drones on with the ongoing monitoring, deep in the waters below life itself flashes and reforms, one creature disappearing into another, rich in numbers and differences, all parts of the wondrous machine.

***Benjamin Neal** is Marine Resources Outreach Associate at the Island Institute.*

Images on page 16-17: Bill Curtsinger (7); Andrew J. Martinez (2); S. Haddock (2)

CENSUS OF MARINE LIFE

Trawl surveys have sometimes been compared to floating over New York City in a balloon and dropping down a collection basket, and then characterizing the life below based on what came back up. The National Marine Fisheries has, through over one hundred years of experience, developed a strict and rigidly followed methodology that improves vastly on this analogy, but the survey, however effective, is still limited only to observations of fish life on the bottom from what is physically collected. With increasing technology, our understanding of the ebb and flow of life beneath the seas is now being augmented through the use of sensing devices that allow an observer on the surface to see and even count organisms while steaming along overhead. Hydro-acoustic and optical devices can be tuned to sense organisms ranging in size from whales to plankton, and can gather information on vastly greater aggregations than could be sampled through collection.

A new and comprehensive collaborative study utilizing some of these new technologies has taken on the vast task of assessing and explaining the diversity, distribution, and abundance of all the world's marine life. This Census of Marine Life has broadly defined its questions as what animals have, do now, and will live in the oceans. With direction and backing from the Alfred P. Sloan Foundation, over 300 of the world's leading ocean scientists have been devising goals and priorities for this immense project. The range of life in the oceans will be identified, measured, and quantified, from larvae to fishes to marine mammals. New species will be sought, and relationships between species will be investigated. Historical and paleo-ecological research will look into the question of changes in populations since human predation became significant, about 500 years ago, and energy flows in current and future fisheries will be pondered.

This global project is just getting underway on what will be an eight- to ten-year investigation. New tools will be used, and new animals may be found, and the inner parts and cogs of the marine world will slowly be brought into greater focus.

For more information visit the census for marine life website at www.http://core.ssc.erc.msstate.edu/senshome.html

Young herring move inshore and up to the surface as evening turns into night. In the morning, as the sun rises and the water warms up, they head back offshore. And the herring weir is the ingenious fisherman's answer to that instinctive behavior.

Bill Curtsinger

TEN TICKS *TO THE* HOGSHEAD

As inshore herring schools decline, a fishing technology from Neolithic times faces extinction too

NAOMI SCHALIT

Visiting a herring weir is a journey into the past. This is a place where fish are measured not in pounds but in "hogsheads," where nets are called "twine" and even the word "weir" is pronounced with an accent that harks back to long-ago England. Make that "ware," not "weer." There's something inexplicably gut-stirring about just seeing the stakes and brush of a weir from the shore, even, perhaps, a visceral evocation of some long lost hunter-gatherer instinct lying latent in all of us.

Weir fishing is a prehistoric method of fishing that by some miracle, and no small amount of regional stubbornness, has persisted, within sight, to this day. And Maynard Morrison — 65 years old, gray haired and with eyes so piercingly blue they could function as lanterns in the dark — well, Maynard Morrison is a piece of that miracle. Because despite all the reasons he shouldn't participate in this vestige of stone-age technology, Morrison has hung onto five weirs — almost half of the remaining weirs in Maine. Not solely because of sentimentality. He's made money from them, lots of money in the past.

But this year could be among the last that Morrison, and the few other self-proclaimed "dinosaurs" who run the other six weirs along the coast, will fish them. The herring just aren't coming in.

Morrison backs his boat trailer confidently down the hill towards the water. He's done it so many times, he's not even looking behind him. Loose gravel crunches and sprays out from under his wheels, and the fiberglass skiff slides easily into the bay. He stops the truck and sets the brake.

"Sure is a pretty morning, what?" he says, hopping down onto the ramp.

Pretty glorious, in fact. It's about seven o'clock and we're on the edge of Gleason's Cove, in Perry, Maine. Perry is a tiny dot on the map along Passamaquoddy Bay, a village where for much of the last century people have made their living from the woods, the fields and the sea. Deer Island sits across the slate-blue reach in front of us, on the other side of the invisible border with Canada. Bald eagles are so commonplace here the local Native Americans get more excited seeing a gray squirrel; the 28-foot tides rush in and out with such force that in some places you can hear them roar. And on this brisk and blindingly sunny fall morning, Maynard Morrison, like his father — who just died — and his father's father before him, is going out to check for herring in his weirs.

Morrison climbs into the boat. "The fish haven't been that plentiful," he says, starting up the engine. "My dad and I were speaking of it before he passed away — he never remembers anything like this, and my grandfather started fishing in 1890."

Morrison speaks with classic downeast understatement — other than a handful early in May, there have been no herring at all in his five weirs this season. Unless things change dramatically in the next year or two, this year could be the beginning of the end of more than a century of weir fishing for his family. And there are only six other weirs being operated in Maine these days. No one else along this coast has seen herring in their weirs either.

"Since 1927, Dad never seen a year that they didn't catch enough to pay the expenses, and he said grandfather never did, either," shouts Morrison over the noise of the engine. "So I guess it's just a fact that the fish are getting quite scarce."

Morrison points the boat toward a line of brush and stakes sticking up out of the water. A gull's-eye view of the weir we're heading to would reveal a long, straight line of stakes called a "leader" running from a shallow, inshore spot, out into a heart-shaped corral of seaweed-covered nets and stakes in deeper water. While Morrison has turned on a well-worn sonar to pick up evidence of herring, there's nothing modern at all about a fishing weir like this or the others dotting the coast. It's a form of hunting that dates back to the Mesolithic era in Europe, and almost as long in North America.

Morrison eyes the blank sonar. "Don't look very encouraging, does it?" he asks. He circles the inside of the weir, and its holding pound in the back. He lets the boat drift, tiny waves nudging it gently. "That's as empty as can be — nothing." He puts the boat into gear.

"We'll go to another one — we've got five!"

As we pass along Perry's sloping green shore, Morrison points out the other weirs. They're all known by their owners. "This is the one that Peter and Angus McPhail fish; this one here, this is the Pottle weir, I usually check it for them." They're all empty — no cormorants or gulls perched on the stakes looking for breakfast, no dots or shapes swimming around on the sonar. Finally, we turn around and head back.

Herring are clannish fish; they swim in great schools. These days, scientists and policy makers spend a lot of time and money trying to figure out the finer points of the behavior of Atlantic herring. But this much has always been known to fishermen like Maynard Morrison: young herring move inshore and up to the surface as evening turns into night. In the morning, as the sun rises and the water warms up, they head back offshore. And the herring weir is the ingenious fisherman's answer to that instinctive behavior.

As they gather along the shore, the fish encounter the weir's long lead line, which acts as a barricade and directs them into the mouth of the heart-shaped or circular impoundment. Once corralled inside, the herring swim around in a figure-eight pattern, and are trapped within when the fisherman closes off the entry point with a net. When it comes time to harvest the fish, a purse seine, gathered at the bottom, pulls them up towards the surface, where in the old days they were hand netted onto waiting boats inside the weir, and in more modern times are vacuum-pumped onto carriers.

The first weirs in Maine were built thousands of years ago by Native Americans. A prehistoric weir was found at the mouth of the Sebasticook River's East Branch in 1991, by amateur archaeologists. Stakes from the weir were subsequently carbon dated and determined to be 5,900 years old. European settlers began building weirs in Maine in the early 19th century. In a 1947 Department of Interior report on the fishing methods of the Maine herring industry, researchers wrote that "the first weirs were rather simple structures of wooden stakes and brush, erected in shallow water in regions where herring were known to be plentiful." Those weirs are almost identical to the ones still standing today, the major difference being that they were originally lined with brush, and now they're lined with nets. These more modern weirs, says University of Maine anthropologist David Sanger, probably owe their ancestry more to European forms of the technology than Native American.

"The whole concept of the herring weir that we see today — Indian people had no such technology," says Sanger. "The kind of thing we see today with the big leader and then going on into the encircled trap, I can't see that as being Native American."

Maynard Morrison's grandfather George built his first weir along the Perry shore in 1889. He was part of a tidal wave of weir building along the Maine coast that was sparked by Frenchman Nicholas Apport's invention in the 1870s of a hermetically sealed tin suitable for canning sardines. Prior to that time, fish were preserved mostly by salting, smoking or drying. In fact, George Morrison initially sold smoked herring to sailing ships that came into Loring's Cove, picked up the barrels and brought them to market in Boston and New York. But that market diminished as the canned sardine market grew. In 1875, the first cannery was built in Eastport, and by 1889, there were 75 factories along the Maine coast. And those factories needed fish.

"The supply of herring at that time was almost inexhaustible," stated Richard

Maynard Morrison's grandfather George built his first weir along the Perry shore in 1889. He was part of a tidal wave of weir building along the Maine coast that was sparked by Frenchman Nicholas Apport's invention in the 1870s of a hermetically sealed tin suitable for canning sardines.

Reed in a history of the Maine sardine industry that he wrote for the official program of the 1949 Lobster Festival. Reed was commissioner of the state's Sea and Shore Fisheries Department, precursor of today's Department of Marine Resources. "Most of the cannery supply was caught in 'brush' weirs in shallow coastal waters. At one time more than a thousand such weirs stretched from Eastport to Lubec."

The early, shallow water weirs were eventually replaced by ones in deeper water where more fish could be caught. Morrison's grandfather moved his further offshore in 1906. Over the years, he maintained that one weir, while Morrison's father worked two.

"But my dad was seeing that he wasn't making quite enough to make it pay, so he built another weir, the one that we build and still have net on today, in Mill Cove.

"In the early days, when my dad was fishing and I was a kid, I can remember every weir had a mooring to hold a seine boat or two, and there'd be a carrier, sometimes two carriers, tied up to every mooring on this shore. It was quite a sight to see all those carriers tied up — 18 canneries in Eastport alone, six or seven in Lubec and Robbinston, Pembroke, this one here in Perry."

Those boats arrived when word got to the canneries that the fish were in. And weir operators, before the days of sonar, had various methods of estimating the number of fish they'd trapped. Morrison says his grandfather used a "feeler line."

"It was Aunt Lydia's thread, tied on to four net leads [weights], and he put it over the side and the fellow in front rowed the boat," says Morrison. As the boat moved around, Morrison's grandfather felt "pings" — or bumps — on the line. A certain number of pings per minute indicated how many hogshead of fish they'd trapped in the weir. "Ten ticks to the hogshead" was the rule of thumb, says Morrison. A hogshead is what canneries called the big barrel they stored the herring in before processing. One hogshead equals 17 and a half bushels.

Weirs were not the only way to catch herring. By the 1940s, faced with the insatiable appetite of canneries that were providing food for soldiers abroad, the more aggressive purse seiners — who could go out and look for schools of herring, not just sit and wait for them to show up — plied the waters. But the canneries liked weir-caught fish. That's because food safety rules dictated that you couldn't can herring that arrived at the canneries with stomachs full of feed — as much of the seine-caught herring did. Weir fishermen had the luxury of allowing the fish to sit in the weir for at least 24 hours, during which they disgorged the feed in their guts. They were "cleaner" fish, and the canneries paid more for them. But even though weirs provided better fish, that didn't stop the canneries from trying to take advantage of weir fishermen, says Morrison.

"There was a problem with the canneries' 'taking measure.' In other words, they'd want two hogsheads for one. This was in the forties. Anyway, the state of Maine says, 'We'll stop this argument,' and they said to the department of weights and measures or something, 'go down,' and they came down and they measured the boats out and they made a mark on the boat about every five hogshead. They'd burn it in, and then they put a seal on it that they had measured the boat and that was the true measurements, and that ended the controversy of taking big measure, or giving short measure."

Almost. Apparently, fishermen also vied for the favor of the canneries as well.

"Lots of times, when fish was real plentiful, one fisherman would say, 'Well, we'll give you a few extra hogsheads if you'll

Christopher Ayres (2)

Maynard Morrison tends the nets at one of his weirs at Gleason's Cove, Perry. "The fish haven't been that plentiful," he says.

Morrison's now down to a handful of weirs. Despite that, in the last few years, he developed a very lucrative new market in New York City. He could sell fresh herring to the Fulton Fish Market for ten times what he got from the remaining three canneries in the area.

come to us,' and that worked like that. The Deer Islanders and Campobello and Grand Mananers, why they was known for giving better measure than the Perry shore."

Over the years, Morrison ran herring carriers as well — a 40 hogshead carrier called the PAUL FREDERICK, and its successor, the CHESTER MARSHALL. And he and his father and brother acquired more and more weirs, many of them "to the west'ard" as he calls it, in Little Machias Bay, South Addison, Frenchman's Bay. By the 1980s, his family had 13 weirs.

Morrison, like many other herring fishermen, stop-seined as well. That's when he flew the coast in a Cessna, looking for schools of herring. Once he found a school, he'd radio to family members and crew who were waiting with dories and nets. They'd travel to a designated corralling spot where they herded the herring and netted them. Sometimes they'd shut off coves where they had weirs, and push them into the weirs; sometimes they'd net them without the weirs. It was a much more efficient way of catching fish.

"The weirs," says Morrison, "we just got to wait patiently until they show up. But we was impatient when we was younger. From 1976 until 1990 we never caught less than a thousand hogshead of fish per year. And our best year, we had 5,200 hogsheads."

But the history of Maine's herring industry is filled with the boom-and-bust cycles typical of other fisheries. A 1931 *Lewiston Journal* headline reads, "The Passamaquoddy Fisherman's Problem — With Ten Months of Employment Reduced to Three and a Pack of Three Million Cases to 400,000, Hundreds Are Moving Away — Fishermen Explain What Struck the Herring Industry In the Bay." In 1939, the *Portland Sunday Telegram's* Herbert Marsh wrote an article entitled "Nearly 7,000 Employed by 25 Canneries — Fisherfolk Dipping 'Silver From Sea.' In 1948, the *Herald* proclaimed, "Sardine Industry Has Seen Immense Growth," while the *Lewiston Journal* asked in 1964, "What's Happening To Our Maine Herring?"

Morrison rode out the ups and downs, and fished his weirs every year. He was able to do that because, like many Mainers, he worked at other jobs, among them a stint in the military in the 1950s. Morrison won't say how much money he made from his weirs, but state fisheries experts say that a good season of weir fishing in the 1990s could have brought in as much as $60,000. But with only three canneries operating in the region now, the market for his kind of fish was drying up. And fewer fish have come in over the past decade. So in the last few years, Morrison stopped building, or re-building, all his weirs.

"They dropped off, one or two at a time. Down there in Frenchman's Bay, Lamoine, that one there was the first to go; that was one of the last to be built, built that for five years. Then, South Addison; we bought a weir from a guy down there, there again those spots there was more spotty — Little Machias Bay, there was an extreme year and we built a couple of years there, but the weir didn't do much after we'd built it."

As the money weirs brought in diminished, the relative cost of maintaining them grew. The nets for one weir alone run $10,000 to $15,000, and Morrison says that if it weren't for the salmon aquaculture industry, he'd have been out of the weir business long ago. That's because every few years, the salmon operations discard the small mesh nets used to keep fish from escaping pens, for fear they will have deteriorated.

"They don't trust them to hold the valuable salmon, but we trust them to hold the herring," he says. So Morrison and the other weir operators around Perry retrieve the nets, cut them up and reassemble them for dressing their weirs.

Morrison's now down to a handful of weirs. Despite that, in the last few years, he developed a very lucrative new market in New York City. He could sell fresh herring to the Fulton Fish Market for ten times what he got from the remaining three canneries in the area. But this year, when the herring failed to show up, he got discouraged.

"There are too many people chasing too few resources," he says. "There just ain't enough fish to go around everywhere like there used to be."

Morrison lays the blame for the herring's disappearance on better technology for catching herring — stop seining, purse seining and pair trawling, the so-called "mobile gear" that allows fishermen to go out and find the herring instead of waiting for the fish to come to them. And the market for herring has changed. No longer is a plate of herring on toast a treat for many Americans. The new herring market is for lobster bait — and the fish don't need to be of the quality a weir produces.

"I've just seen that there's more efficient methods of catching them and more people catching them, more boats rigging all the time. They're just being overfished as far as I'm concerned."

Others don't think the herring are necessarily being over-exploited. Dave Libby, chief herring biologist for the state, says there are still herring out there to be caught. They're just not coming inshore.

"Why it happened we still don't know. It could have been a change in environment, change in fish behavior for some reason, large predators like whales or tuna aren't driving them inshore, the water temperature could have changed." Libby shakes his head, and edges towards some agreement with Morrison.

"And then we get to fishing pressure — where it was too much fishing pressure on these fish, and just caused them to leave the coast and go to the outer banks."

But it doesn't really matter to Morrison why the fish aren't here. He's undressed all his weirs from the past year, and only plans to operate three of the five during the 2001 season. And if those don't catch herring, then he's finished building weirs. "I don't plan to have any five years from now," he says.

And sitting in his kitchen, in a house built on property his grandfather bought in 1889, Maynard Morrison leans his elbows on the kitchen table, rests his chin on his hands and turns away from the view through a huge window behind him.

"Maybe it's time to retire," he says.

In back of him, on the other side of the glass, is the Perry shore — where for several generations and many dozens of years, the herring schooled up on summer evenings and found their way into Morrison weirs.

***Naomi Schalit** is a reporter for Maine Public Radio.*

In the old days, fish in a weir were netted into waiting boats. In more modern times they were vacuum pumped into carriers.

Christopher Ayres (2)

In the Lair of
THE ICE KING

OPEN WATER IN THE HIGH ARCTIC CARRIES A MESSAGE FOR THE REST OF THE WORLD

PHILIP CONKLING

Photographs by Gary Comer

CROSSING THE GREENLAND SEA JULY 13-15, 2000

As our vessel cruises north from Iceland, it is hard to keep track of time when there is no difference between day and night. Most of us sleep throughout the night-time hours with the portholes covered to block out the white light while our highly competent crew moves TUMOIL, a 151-foot cruising vessel, through the Greenland Sea round the clock. It has been overcast and cool for most of the week since leaving Reykjavik, Iceland's largest port, where we met Gary Comer, TURMOIL's owner, and the crew. We are on the adventure of a lifetime — a voyage that will traverse the remote western coast of Iceland, then cross the Greenland and Norwegian Seas for a landfall at Spitsbergen, one of the most remote islands in the northern seas. Our intentions are to explore the fringes of the known world where few are able to go and to record our impressions of the life of the sea north of the Arctic Circle.

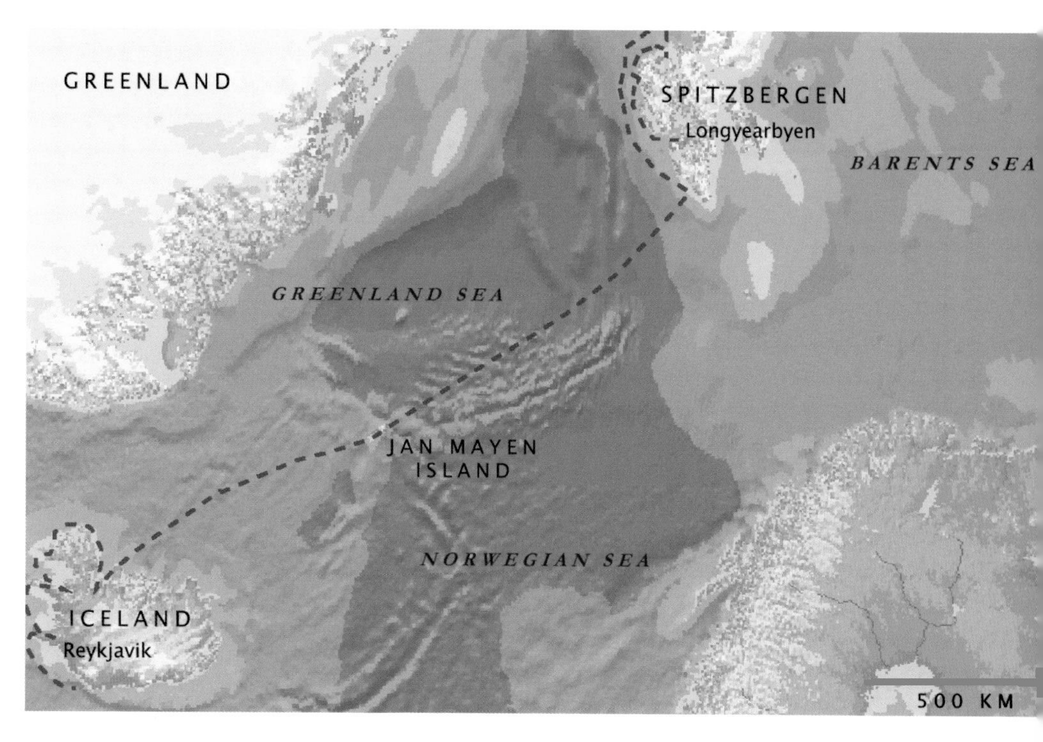

TURMOIL crossed the Greenland Sea from Reykjavik to Spitzbergen.

Throughout the day, the ship's routine goes on smoothly and unceasingly. TURMOIL's four passengers find little corners in the library, the main saloon or the bridge to catch up on reading or to send e-mails back home. The satellite coverage for regular telecommunications gets patchy north of 70 degrees latitude, so today may be our last contact with our offices and families back in Maine.

It is truly amazing, of course, that we can communicate so effortlessly through written messages from the middle of the Greenland Sea, and perhaps a little frightening how emotionally dependent you can get on the technology if it is available. But the technology is indisputably useful. Neil Emmott, first mate, has some kind of skin rash that has bothered him for some time and is not improving. So our captain, Philip Walsh, takes digital pictures of Neil's condition. To get a diagnosis, he sends the pictures attached to an e-mail to a service out of Miami called Maritime Medicine. A few hours later a doctor's message suggests a bacterial infection that should be treated with a topical antibiotic that proves to be successful. Later Gary Comer loses a filling and then the tooth that held it, but as yet the Worldwide Web offers no replacement (at least that we can find) for this predicament.

The weather reports also come in via electronic telecommunication either on the fax or e-mail server. The service is called Fleet Weather, based in New York. Philip Walsh sends Fleet Weather our position plus visibility, sea condition and barometric pressure, and gets back a 36-hour forecast each day. Fleet Weather's forecasts are uncannily precise. The recent forecast, for instance, was for winds to be southeast at 12 knots, backing into the east at 2 p.m. for six hours and then dropping to below 5 knots. The winds did exactly as predicted.

The weather continues to improve throughout the afternoon and we all gather on the stern deck before supper. There is a moderately thick cloud cover overhead, although the horizon is clear all the way around the compass. Soon even the clouds overhead begin to dissipate. Then suddenly just off the stern quarter is a massive spout and then the long dark back of an enormous creature from the underworld emerges from the troughs in the waves. It can only be a blue whale. It surfaces once more, further off, and is then is lost in our wake as we continue our northerly course. Shortly afterwards the captain spots a tall straight silhouette many miles out that he at first mistakes for a sailboat mast. We alter course by 30 degrees to investigate. It takes us a quarter of an hour to get in the vicinity and suddenly we are surrounded by whale spouts exploding off to port and starboard.

As we angle closer in, a pair of finbacks, identified by white chevrons on their starboard sides, surfaces right off our beam. They are feeding on fish that have come to the surface. Soon two other finbacks join them as we steam side by side at ten knots, approximating their speed. Every minute or so they burst to the surface in an explosion of spume and foam that cascades off their glistening dark backs. Then the most remarkable spectacle unfolds as three of the whales burst to surface almost touching each other, their torsos silver in the spray. One whale's mouth is so wide open

its baleen plates are plainly visible. They lunge after a shoal of invisible fish, probably herring, then twist on their sides extending flippers vertically in the air. Seconds later the tip of one the flukes trails by like an enormous shark fin knifing through the water. The "lunge feeding" goes on and on, as the whales chase the fish and feed. The noise of the spouts is deep and otherworldly, a cross between a shout of exuberance and a moan of despair. It is nearly 11 p.m. when we break off from the whales, but the sun is still several points above the horizon. Tonight the sun will not dip below the horizon at all, but will roll around the rim like a giant yellow marble balanced on the lip of an enormous saucer until it slowly begins to ascend on the other side of due north.

POLAR ICE AT THE 80TH PARALLEL
JULY 19, 2000

After a quiet night in a fjord at the northern end of Spitsbergen we awake to gradually clearing skies. TURMOIL heads north from her anchorage with the intention of exploring the edge of the sea ice where we might see polar bears hunting for seals. As the clouds continue to lift in the shimmering morning sunlight, we begin to see mirages of ice off to starboard. A fata morgana, a mirage that appears in polar regions caused by air temperature and density differences, now fills the entire eastern horizon looming up like a vertical wall through the binoculars. This can only be the edge of the pack ice, although it looks like the edge of an ice escarpment — a barrier no one would ever be able to cross.

Soon we are nosing through what the captain calls a field of "bergy bits," little pieces of ice dotting the surface. A mile further ahead we swivel into the edge of pack ice. When we arrive, Gary calls for the jet boat so we can maneuver through the floating bergs and get a closer look at the ice field swaying on gentle Arctic swells. Meanwhile puffins careen by overheard, seemingly flying through the rigging of TURMOIL. The sun glints silver off the shifting ice pack. The sound of the pack ice is like a rushing wind off in the distance, as the heave and surge of the sea lifts and lowers a thousand square miles of restless ice that shifts uneasily against itself like a huge, moaning diaphone. It is the dull roar from the lair of the ice king.

A short while later, back aboard TURMOIL in the pilothouse, there is a brief celebration at the GPS station as we cross the 80th parallel. Only 600 miles to the Pole! For one mad moment, the same thought flashes across all our minds; maybe we will get lucky and find a long enough lead through the ice pack to make a dash for the Pole and get to the top of the world! Only for a moment, though. Who in his right mind would risk this boat for such an ice-crazed dream? But still…

FLYING OVER THE GREENLAND ICE SHEET JULY 23, 2000

Our voyage ended, TURMOIL puts into the port of Longyearbyen on Spitsbergen's western coast where we will meet the plane that will take us back to the temperate world. It is a clear morning as we take off and re-cross the empty expanse of the Greenland Sea we had traversed in TURMOIL a week earlier. In less than a half an hour the plane is over the eastern edge of Greenland, a half continent-sized island almost completely obscured by an immense blanket of ice and snow. The morning sun pools in pockets of golden glow over the frigid waters at the white edge of the land. This eastern edge of Greenland is seemingly discharging bits of its frozen surface into the southerly trending currents that carry this flotilla of icebergs south, like an endless stream of packing bits loosed in the wind.

THE VIEW BACK HOME

Several weeks after returning from the TURMOIL voyage we were stunned, like many others, to read a front-page story in the New York Times reporting that a Russian icebreaker, YAMAL, had left Spitsbergen with a group of tourists in mid-August headed for the Pole. When they got there a week later, instead of ice, they discovered nothing but open water. There were several American scientists leading the tourist expedition aboard the YAMAL, including Dr. James McCarthy, an oceanographer and director of the Museum of Comparative Zoology at Harvard University.

McCarthy said that he had been at the Pole six years earlier and had encountered a completely frozen sheet of ice. This time, he reported, he had never seen so much open water in the polar region. The Captain of the YAMAL said he had been making this passage for the past decade and generally had to cut through an ice sheet six to nine feet thick. (Other reports from prominent polar scientists published a few weeks later pointed out that approximately ten percent of the polar Arctic region is open water, since the ice pack constantly shifts in winds and currents to create pockets of open ocean, and that open water will appear from time to time at the Pole.)

Despite such disagreement, the evidence is mounting that an unusual amount of melting is occurring in the polar regions of the North Atlantic. What effects this might have on the rest of the ocean, including our small window on the world at the edge of the Gulf of Maine, is anyone's guess.

What we know is that the earth's surface temperature, including the temperature of the sea's surface, has increased by about one degree since the late 19th century, and that the 1990s have been the warmest decade on record. The difference in average global temperatures between a full-

fledged ice age and our present interglacial climate is only about five degrees, so this global temperature increase is cause for concern, if not alarm. We also know from detailed recent measurements that the southern half of the Greenland ice sheet, the second largest ice sheet in the world after Antarctica, has shrunk substantially in the last five years. Greenland is losing ice at a rate comparable to the size of Maryland covered by a foot of ice melting per year. Finally, measurements by the U.S. Navy, from submarine logs of voyages under the Pole, also reveal that the ice layer is substantially thinner than it used to be.

Closer to home, a story from last summer, perhaps insignificant in the global scheme of things, is a reminder of how interconnected life in the ocean can be. As part of the Penobscot Bay Marine Collaborative, the Island Institute administers an interdisciplinary team of scientists, fishermen and managers trying to understand the dynamics of lobsters in the bay. Part of the project is to place college graduate "Island Fellows" and interns aboard lobster boats to collect information from cooperating fishermen. Lobstermen know that every year the habits of the world's most favored crustacean will be somewhat different than the previous year. Since anyone can remember, lobstermen in the spring have begun to set traps close to shore to intercept lobsters as they crawl into shallower, warmer waters to shed their old shells and breed. But last year was dramatically different. Fishermen set their gear as always, but catches in April, May and early June were not just low, especially in the Midcoast — they were almost non-existent. Already nervous because of the collapse of lobster population in Long Island Sound, N.Y., Maine fishermen feared the worst.

Then, beginning in early June, a strange thing happened. Lobstermen began catching shedders, very large numbers of them, between three and four weeks earlier than normal. And many of the lobsters with new shells were caught in deeper water than usual. The evidence is anecdotal and therefore "unscientific," but a picture emerges: the early part of the lobster season was dramatically different from what many established fishermen had ever observed.

Informal observations from many sources also suggest that the deeper bottom waters along the eastern and midcoast section of Maine were unusually warm early in the season, a state of affairs that led to an unusually early shed. Assuming that these observations prove to be accurate, the question is why warm bottom waters entered the bays of eastern and midcoast Maine, and what this change may be telling us about circulation patterns in the Gulf of Maine and beyond.

GLOBAL OCEAN CURRENTS AND CIRCULATION

Mariners have been studying ocean currents for centuries, but systematic observations of global ocean circulation features began in the mid-19th century

GOMOOS

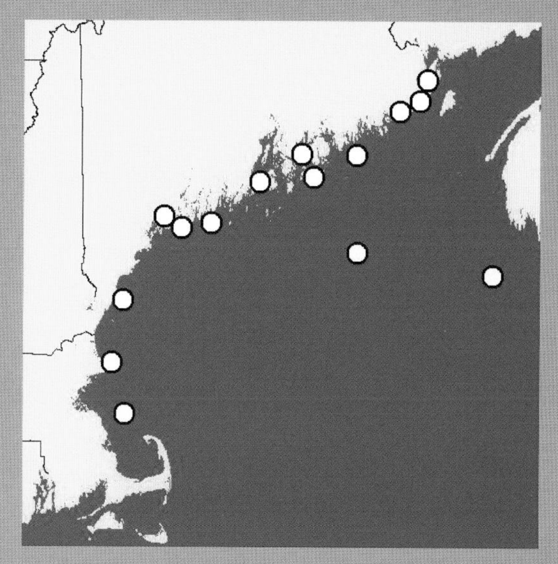

Proposed monitoring locations in the Gulf of Maine

Fishermen talk to each other about whether the ocean is warmer or cooler this season from the last and speculate on what that might mean for harvests. Mariners tune into weather radio frequencies straining to get the latest wind and wave forecasts. Shippers and their marine pilots need to know how surface currents might affect their navigation in tight channels. And everyone wants to know when and where coastal fogs will spread a gray blanket over our senses. The trouble is that specific information about these and dozens of other kinds of marine information is exceedingly spotty and hard to come by. But that is about to change in a big way for the Gulf of Maine.

As an outgrowth of Governor Angus King's focus on increasing Maine's investment in marine technology and with the leadership from Maine's senior Senator, Olympia Snowe in Washington, the Gulf of Maine has been selected as the first-in-the-nation test bed to take the vital signs of our oceanic region. The Gulf of Maine Ocean Observing System (GOMOOS) is a new organization that has been created by a unique collaboration of users to manage this new system. GOMOOS will deploy and report data from 15 oceanographic buoys, four shore-based radar stations and a variety of orbiting satellite sensors to provide users with "real-time" information on the ecological pulse of the Gulf of Maine. Wave height and frequency, wind speed, barometric pressure, air temperature, surface and subsurface current directions and fog conditions are only a few of the measurements that GOMOOS will collect and post on its web site with regular and frequent updates.

Evan Richert, the President of the Board of Trustees of GOMOOS, likens the organization to a utility owned by its members, that supplies data to the general public. Founding members of the Board include a unique cross section of government agencies such as the Massachusetts Water Resources Authority which manages Boston's huge waste water system to private interests such as Irving Oil, Portland Pipeline, and the James Sewall Co, which specializes in environmental mapping technology. Nonprofit members such as the New England and Gulf of Maine Aquariums and the Island Institute will benefit from being able to present new educational materials for their members and visitors. Fisheries organizations will benefit not only with up-to-the hour weather forecasts, but with data on how and where temperature features in the Gulf from the sea floor to the surface may affect harvesting strategies.

Although the initial infrastructure is made possible by an up front investment of $6.5 million of federal funds, the salary of GOMOOS' executive director, Dr. Philip Bogden, is paid out of membership dues. Annual dues range from a low of $500 for small organizations such as the Maine Lobsterman's Association to a high of $10,000 for larger organizations such as Bath Iron Works and Woods Hole Oceanographic Institution. University of Maine, Bigelow Laboratory, University of New Hampshire, and Bedford Institute of Oceanography in Nova Scotia are all collaborating on the initial design and deployment of the system. For more information and hourly wind, wave and weather information see www.gomoos.org.

—Philip W. Conkling

when Matthew Fontaine Maury, Oceanographer of the United States Navy, began to collect comprehensive current observations from fishing and commercial fleets operating throughout the world's oceans. These observations were painstakingly compiled to provide ship captains with estimates of the speed and direction of major ocean currents. Captains contributed information because no one could even begin to see the whole picture of the North Atlantic, for instance. It was only through cooperation over many years that major features could be mapped.

One of the most important ocean currents is the Gulf Stream that trends northerly off eastern North America to the region south of the Grand Banks of Newfoundland. From there it flows eastward across the North Atlantic. The significance of the Gulf Stream was not lost on commercial shippers, who laid their courses to take advantage of or reduce the disadvantage of this huge river-like current.

But there is an even more important relationship between the Gulf Stream and climate. We know that London and Paris, on the eastern edge of the North Atlantic, are at the same latitude as Nain, Labrador, and St. John's, Newfoundland, on the Atlantic's western side. London and Paris are temperate because of the influence of the warm waters of the Gulf Stream, which releases heat to the overlying air masses to create a warmer climate. Meanwhile Nain and St. John's are subarctic because the cold currents that grip their shores create cold air masses that chill not just the bones, but the whole surrounding landscape. What is relatively new here is knowledge of how tightly coupled ocean circulation and climate actually are, throughout all the world's major oceans.

The Gulf Stream can be viewed as a vital moving piece of a global thermostat that transports heat trapped in equatorial oceans northward toward the poles. Because much of the rainfall over North America is intercepted by mountains and falls on land, the saltiness of the Gulf Stream is high, relative to other ocean surface waters. As this salty and therefore heavy seawater flows north, it is cooled by winter winds in the region south of Iceland, and it sinks. Although tongues of the Gulf Stream continue to flicker north (including along the western coast of Spitsbergen), most of this dense, cold water sinks to the abyssal depths of the North Atlantic. There it sets up a giant, deepwater conveyor system that flows along the bottom of the Atlantic basin beyond the tip of Africa, all the way to the edge of the Antarctic shelf.

Off Antarctica, North Atlantic bottom water, called the North Atlantic Conveyor, meets sinking cold surface water trapped beneath the sea ice to form a deep raceway around the Antarctic continent. The cold bottom waters of the North Atlantic Conveyor vie for dominance with the bottom waters that descend from underneath the Antarctic ice sheet. Currently the North Atlantic Conveyor is slightly dominant and forms the source of salty bottom currents that flow through deep topographic passages to drive the circulation systems of both the Pacific and Indian Oceans.

The world's northernmost active volcano, Haaken Toppen, rises over 7,000 feet at Jan Mayen Island.

But what happens if the North Atlantic Conveyor loses its dominance? Perhaps no one has given this question as much thought as the dean of American oceanographers, Wallace Broecker of Columbia University. Referring to the analysis of Greenland ice cores where a detailed record of the earth's climate during the past 60,000 years has been unraveled, Broecker points to clear evidence that the earth's climate has switched back and forth between two modes of operation. The difference in time between interglacial epochs of moderate climate, and periods of intense cold is measured on a time scale of a few decades to a few years. How can such gigantic shifts in the earth's climate occur on such short notice? Scientists like Broecker do not know for

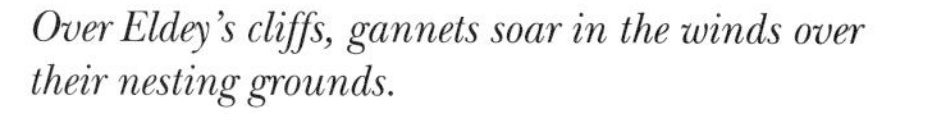

Over Eldey's cliffs, gannets soar in the winds over their nesting grounds.

sure, but the most sophisticated climate models suggest the "trigger" is a shift in ocean circulation.

Broecker reasons that slight changes in the relative strength of the two major sources of bottom water in the North Atlantic or the Antarctic shelf can trigger a rapid reorganization of global ocean circulation. This analysis suggests the only physical mechanism that can explain a decrease in the rate of North Atlantic bottom water production results from a reduction in saltiness, and hence density, of its surface waters. Thus, if rapid increases in the rate of melting of Greenland ice cap and the Arctic pack ice were to occur, the resulting fresh water increase in the eastern North Atlantic would reduce the dominance of the North Atlantic Conveyor. With even a moderate weakening, the deep ocean circulation patterns can flip into their other mode of operation where the Antarctic bottom waters are dominant. The resulting ocean circulation alters global weather patterns, including the strength and direction of the Gulf Stream. The Gulf Stream no longer flickers as far to the north in the eastern North Atlantic, quickly plunging northern Europe into a much colder climate. The resulting change in atmospheric circulation leads to new storm centers that transport more water vapor to the poles. As water vapor builds up at the poles, ice sheets begin to creep outward, but the persistent storms also reduce the saltiness and density of the waters that previously drove the North Atlantic Conveyor.

While we do not know whether the North Atlantic Conveyor is slowing enough to risk major changes in global ocean circulation and global climate, major ice melting in the eastern North Atlantic is an observed fact. The changes in bottom water temperatures in the Gulf of Maine can (and will be) documented as either a trend or an anomaly.

No one has definitely linked the melting of ice in the high Arctic to the production of greenhouse gases released by the burning of fossil fuels, but it is worth asking what kind of worldwide experiment is now ineluctably underway. Global warming scientists used to model a doubling of greenhouse gases in the earth's atmosphere and try to interpret the results. Newer projections make a tripling of the volume of greenhouse gases ever more likely during the 21st century.

Those with their hands on the levers of government, at least on this side of the North Atlantic, have taken a "wait and see" approach to the debate over whether global warming is real and a cause for concern. Because scientists are unable to predict with any certainty the timing and magnitude of global climate change, nor even whether it will produce new deserts or new ice ages, some might think this strategy has the prudence of Solomon. But if you view the doubling or tripling of heat-trapping gases in the atmosphere to a global game of Russian roulette, especially when the outcome is so unpredictable, the strategy looks less like Solomon's and more like Nero's.

Philip Conkling is president of the Island Institute. James Essex, Island Fellow, assisted in the preparation of this article.

Red seals, which have never been hunted, trail their flippers out behind, while fur seals, prized for their soft coats, have forward facing flippers.

HIGH FLIGHT, COMMON SENSE

IN 1925, MAINE EXPLORER DONALD MACMILLAN PROVIDED A CRITICAL PLATFORM FOR PIONEERING EXPERIMENTS IN AVIATION AND RADIO

DAVID D. PLATT

Peary-MacMillan Arctic Museum (9)

Donald MacMillan's schooner BOWDOIN at Wiscasset in June, 1925, just prior to her departure for the Arctic.

Donald MacMillan, 1925

In early June, 1925, a U.S. Navy cruiser steamed up the Sheepscot River to Wiscasset where Donald MacMillan was preparing to depart for Labrador and northern Greenland aboard his schooner, the BOWDOIN. The cruiser had been dispatched from Boston on orders of the Secretary of the Navy. She carried a large radio transmitter that had been taken from the battleship TEXAS and which the secretary was determined to place in MacMillan's hands for his upcoming trip.

MacMillan had enlisted the Navy's help in organizing his 1925 effort and was in no position, it would seem, to question the Navy's wisdom about radio communications. But the BOWDOIN and the other expedition vessel, the steamer PEARY, were already burdened with food and fuel, three dismantled Navy airplanes and their pilots and mechanics, several spare airplane engines and wings, as well as shortwave radio sets and other up-to-date equipment that was to be tested on the trip. Even on deck, space was very tight and the TEXAS transmitter, MacMillan and his men felt, simply wasn't needed. They had already declined to take it aboard when they were at the Charlestown Navy Yard in Boston, and at the risk of insulting his Navy sponsors, MacMillan sailed away from Wiscasset, again leaving it behind.

The BOWDOIN in Greenland, 1925.

The Navy's enthusiasm for its bulky "spark set" was undiminished. A week later when MacMillan had reached Sydney, Nova Scotia, a destroyer showed up, again carrying the big transmitter, this time with an ultimatum from Navy secretary Curtis Wilbur: install it on the BOWDOIN or the PEARY, or else.

"If I failed to do this," MacMillan wrote in his journal, "all navy equipment and aviators and mechanics were to be returned to Washington." So he instructed the destroyer's captain to load the transmitter aboard the PEARY and to inform the secretary that it had been delivered. The captain promised to send the message in the evening. "And why in the evening?" MacMillan asked, knowing the answer. "In sending messages over such a long distance," the captain replied, "we can always do better at night."

Then, as MacMillan tells it, "It occurred to me to request the captain to bring his message over to the BOWDOIN, and have my radio operator send it at once ... the captain of the government ship brought to the BOWDOIN his message. John Reinhartz, my radio operator, called up a boy in Washington, D.C. He received the message ... walked down the street to the Navy office on Constitution Avenue, and personally handed it to Secretary Wilbur!"

The little trick MacMillan and Reinhartz had played on the captain and his superior (who did not withdraw his support after all) was a demonstration of something youthful ham radio operators all over the world already knew, even in 1925: that shortwave communication had far greater reach than the older "longwave" system the Navy was using worldwide at the time, and that unlike it, shortwave could be reliable both day and night.

The 1925 MacMillan arctic expedition would again prove this to be true, just as it would demonstrate the value of airplanes for polar exploration and the need to organize arctic travel in a whole new way. Indeed, MacMillan and his collaborators, the Navy and the National Geographic Society, had embarked on an effort that would transform arctic exploration from dogsleds to something entirely different.

As for the fate of the Navy's obsolete transmitter, MacMillan hazarded a guess: "I never saw it again," he wrote in his journal. "Only one thing could have happened — the men threw it overboard."

Three men — MacMillan, Lt. Richard E. Byrd of the Navy and Eugene F. McDonald, president of the Zenith Radio Corporation — were the dominant figures in the 1925 expedition. Others, including the president of the National Geographic Society, participated in portions of the trip — a National Geographic photographer on the expedition took the first color photographs in the far north on August 25, 1925 — but MacMillan, Byrd and McDonald were aboard its ships, capturing the attention of the outside world via short-wave broadcasts, flying its experimental airplanes. Circumstances — the year 1925 would turn out to be the coldest on record, for one thing — prevented them from achieving all of their objectives, but the trip broke important new ground. It was, in the words of one account, "the first modern polar expedition."

POLITICS

Planning, or more accurately, political maneuvering for the 1925 expedition had begun late the previous winter. The Navy had been interested in sending a blimp, the SHENANDOAH, over the North Pole, and had picked Byrd as navigator before scrapping the idea. On his own, Byrd had been working to line up private support for an expedition, but with limited success. MacMillan and McDonald, meanwhile, had been working with the National

E-Took-A-Shoo with kayak paddle, expedition planes behind.

The steamer PEARY *was chartered for the 1925 expedition, and carried extra supplies including the three Loening amphibian aircraft that would make aviation history.*

Geographic Society on a plan to test Zenith's latest short-wave radio equipment in the Arctic. In February, 1925, MacMillan and McDonald met with the Secretary of the Navy to ask for an amphibian aircraft to explore Baffin Island and the Greenland Icecap that summer. Exploring by air, they told the secretary, would allow them to explore inland areas heretofore only accessible by dogsled.

The result, after some maneuvering involving a Maine senator and President Calvin Coolidge, was support from the Navy, with the understanding that its man, Byrd, would join the expedition and be in charge of the Navy personnel attached to it. The expedition was to be equipped with three Loening Amphibian aircraft, courtesy of the Navy.

The arrangement necessitated an uneasy joining of three powerful personalities. MacMillan brought experience and seamanship dating back to Robert Peary's 1908 polar expedition; McDonald was a successful entrepreneur, having made a fortune selling cars, who founded Zenith Radio; while Byrd contributed his unshakable belief in aviation's promise to polar exploration in the 20th century. That the three didn't always get along is an understatement — backbiting that had begun in Washington, D.C., the previous winter continued during the trip north and for years afterward as each sought to define the expedition's successes and failures as he saw them.

AVIATION

The three planes that went north on the deck of the PEARY in 1925 were the latest thing, literally: the prototype had had its maiden flight less than a year earlier. The amphibians lent to the Naval Arctic Unit of the MacMillan expedition actually belonged to the Army, which seems — at a time of intense interservice rivalry — to have been ordered by the President to make them available. As a design they were somewhat problematical. Their engine, the "Liberty" design developed during World War I, had to be installed upside down so as to allow visibility from the cockpit. While the engines were adapted for the purpose, they did experience problems during the expedition, some stemming from inadequate lubrication. Still, these fragile-looking, open-cockpit aircraft allowed Byrd and his team to glimpse territory never before viewed by men who hadn't gone there on foot. Making use of limited open water, they took off and landed dozens of times and ventured for the first time over Ellesmere Island and the Polar Sea.

The exploits of the expedition's aviators, commanded by Byrd, are a recurring theme in the handwritten journal MacMillan kept during the 1925 expedition. Their three aircraft, designated "NA1," "NA2" and "NA3," were offloaded onto a steep beach at Etah harbor to be assembled. This was on Greenland's northwest coast in late July; by August 3 they were ready to fly.

National Geographic Society

The airplanes were carried on deck without their wings and had to be assembled on the beach at Etah, Greenland.

MacMillan the arctic veteran (the 1925 trip was his fourth journey north of the Arctic Circle) was clearly convinced of the planes' value. But he couldn't resist dwelling on the risks associated with flying untried aircraft in country whose dangers he knew well, and wherever experience told him a problem might occur, he could be counted on to come up with a time-tested solution, usually reflecting his respect for local knowledge.

ETAH, AUG. 3: *The NA3 was launched this afternoon. [We] motored up the fjord to an Eskimo rock-sod … house and tipik (sealskin tent) in order to obtain my new bear skin pants. I may say that [while] such are not a necessary garment during the summer months, there was a possibility that we might be compelled to land on the ice of the Polar Sea. In the event of a forced landing in such inhospitable surroundings, polar bear skin pants, common among the men of the Smith Sound tribe, might be of help…*

Returning from this outing, MacMillan was offered a flight, presumably wearing his new pants. He, a Navy pilot and a mechanic "had the distinction of being the first to fly the Arctic in this area…" Characteristically, the reaction of his Eskimo friends is what interests him most.

We "hopped off" and flew up the fjord to the ice-cap, and circled over Alida Lake at a height of 1,000 feet. We waved to the Eskimos as we went by their tent. One can imagine their feelings. This was the first plane which they had ever seen, and ours the first plane to enter the American Arctic.

A new age in Arctic exploration had dawned, and MacMillan could appreciate (and celebrate) the significance of what he had witnessed. Still, the innate caution that would allow him to sail thousands of uncharted miles along the Labrador and Greenland coasts on more than two dozen trips to the region seems to have made him prudent, if not downright gloomy, about aviation's supposed benefits.

AUG. 5, 1925: *Planes in the air all day, now and then flying pretty well out over Smith Sound. It is of considerable interest to note that minor troubles have developed in all of them — a serious affair here in the far north…*

Entries for the succeeding days and weeks record other problems as the pilots made repeated efforts to transport gasoline and supplies to several spots closer to the Polar Sea. The idea was to increase the expedition's range by allowing the planes to land and refuel, just as earlier explorers in the Arctic and Antarctic had sent dog teams ahead to place caches of food. The shortcomings of this approach became obvious after several attempts: the amount of open water available for landings and takeoffs was severely limited because of ice, and the ice on the Polar Sea itself was far too rough to serve as a runway.

AUG. 6: *Two planes were loaded to the limit with gas for the Ellesmere Land trip. Neither one could get off the water, therefore the trip was given up for the day.*

NA1 installing a new engine. Bearing burned out. Miserable weather, rain and fog. I placed the BOWDOIN alongside of the PEARY, and hoisted one of the new Liberty Motors to her deck.

This type of engine is not suited to be used on the Loening Amphibian Plane, for the simple reason that the propeller cannot function without hitting the for'ard deck of the plane. Therefore to enable the engine to do its work, it is necessary to turn the engine upside down! This we have done, although we realize that by so doing we have seriously interfered with the oiling system. Such was a serious oversight on the part of Lieutenant Byrd, who selected this type of plane. They plainly do not have the required range to reach the vast unexplored area of the Polar Sea, the margin of which I reached with dog teams in 1914.

MacMillan kept observing and reporting on the activities of his local Eskimo friends who, not surprisingly, were intrigued by all the mechanized goings-on. He found their reactions as interesting as anything Byrd and his pilots were accomplishing in the air.

AUG. 8: *Koo-e-tig-I-to and Metik walk down from Anoritok to satisfy their curiosity in regard to the huge birds in the air, which they have seen lately, and have heard distinctly. When heard for the first time, they thought it must be the sound of falling rocks, a sound which reverberates through the hills, especially in the spring when huge blocks fall from above to the talus below. It might be, they thought, the sound of an earthquake, which always prompted them to paddle rapidly for the shore. And then the day when they actually saw one of our planes in the sky! Only one decision — hike down to Etah to satisfy their curiosity.*

Eventually even Byrd seems to have become frustrated with the planes' performance and the risk that a plane might go down in a remote area. MacMillan, more familiar with on-the-ground conditions and survival in the Arctic, takes a more confident stance.

MacMillan supported the 1925 expedition's technological goals, but the friends he made in Arctic communities always came first.

AUG. 9: ... *at a conference at noon today, Commander Byrd stated that he considered it highly dangerous for us to fly over Ellesmere land; that a man had absolutely no chance for his life if an engine went dead. His opinion was shared by our best aviator, Carl Reber, and our best mechanic, Charlie Rocherville. On the contrary, Lieutenant Schur [one of the Navy pilots] agreed with me that there were many places where we might have landed between here and Flagler Bay.*

We have decided to make another flight in an attempt to reach Bay Fjord, and a possible place for landing.

The goal, they decided, would be a house that had been built by the Canadian government to store emergency supplies. The house could become a forward base as well as an emergency haven in the event of disaster.

AUG. 10: ... *Byrd thought that it might be a good idea to see this house, since it might be our salvation in the event of a forced landing in Ellesmere Land. It might be the means of saving our lives. He also suggested that it might be used for radio tests between our equipment here and the station in Ellesmere Land. He therefore left for Cape Sabine during the afternoon.*

MacMillan and Schur took a reconnaissance flight along the coast to check on ice and take pictures. Again, they made contact with the locals.

We went on down the coast as far as Igd-lu-da-houny, where we found a large group of Eskimos. The sand beach was so inviting that we ran the plane right up until it grounded. All the Eskimos rushed to the beach, and gathered around with various exclamations of wonder and surprise. After distributing many presents, we pushed off and started back in slightly foggy weather, flying out around Cape Alexander. On the way down we flew over the Crystal Palace and Cape Alexander glaciers.

What he and Schur saw from the air seems to have prompted MacMillan to begin considering the expedition's options. Ice extended further south than usual in 1925, and MacMillan had no intention of becoming stuck for the winter. He put his concerns into a formal communication to Byrd:

I wrote a letter to Byrd tonight, in fact, two letters, one outlining our course of retreat in case of accident to the planes, and one requesting information as to the ability of the planes to put us out on the Polar Sea. I doubt very much of our ability to reach the unexplored area north-west of Axel Heiberg Land with the Loening Amphibian Planes.

Local Eskimos participated in shipboard broadcasts from Greenland during July and August, proving the value of shortwave radio as a global communications medium. Listeners included a 15-year-old boy in Cedar Rapids, Iowa, who reported hearing the group's voices distinctly. MacMillan is seated at right; Eugene F. McDonald of Zenith Radio stands at right.

MacMillan's doubts didn't prevent him from participating in what must have been an amazing flight the next day, over Ellesmere island's ice cap in the company of Byrd and Navy pilots M.A. Schur, Earl Reber and Floyd Bennett. It was the expedition's most ambitious day of flying in its open-cockpit planes, literally a chancy piece of barnstorming over an Arctic wasteland.

AUG. 11: *Left today at 11:50 a.m. in company with NA1 and NA3 for Bay Fjord. We passed over a large sheet of ice in Smith Sound and directly over the centre of Bedford Island at an altitude of 3,500 feet. From the island on up we could see open water at the head of Alexander Fiord and Hayes Fjord. Flagler Bay was practically clear. The valley did not look a bit inviting if our engine stopped, therefore the pilots decided to take their chances on the ice-cap.*

We climbed to a height of 5,000 feet in order to get over the glaciers. When half way across Ellesmere Land, heavy clouds gathered ahead of us, covering up everything. Beneath the clouds we could see patches of open water in Bay Fjord. We lost Reber in the NA3 and turned back to "pick him up." Within a few minutes he had disappeared again. Acting under orders from Byrd, who really was in charge of the planes, Schur, my pilot, turned back when he realized there was no possibility of getting down through the clouds to a safe landing. To my surprise Bennett and Byrd passed us and went on.

We now climbed to 6,000 feet, and flew directly over the summit of the highest ice cap to Bierstadt Fjord, which was entirely free of ice.

MacMillan and Schur did spot the government house from the air before they turned around and headed for the ships.

... I instructed Schur to circle down to an altitude of about 1,000 feet to give me an opportunity to see the house built and left by the Canadian Government, which, I understand, is filled with food. We found it in the small harbor, occupied by the FRAM in 1898-99. Fram Haven, I believe it is called.

Upon our arrival in Etah we found to our surprise Reber in the NA3 tied up to the PEARY. *He had trouble in getting altitude when passing over Ellesmere Land, and turned back. Byrd and Bennett came in ten minutes later.*

Byrd reported that winds had prevented him from landing on Ellesmere. He told MacMillan, in answer to his letter of two days earlier, that he'd like to try landing supplies at a spot called Flagler Bay. Reluctantly, MacMillan approved.

AUG. 14: *The NA1 and the NA3 got away today, and succeeded in landing 100 gallons of gas at the head of Flagler Bay — something we should have done at the very beginning of our operations, had I known of the extremely [limited] supply on each plane. The two planes left again tonight, but were unable to land, due to a heavy sea, driven into the bay by an easterly wind and also by bits of drift ice, which might easily punch a hole in each ship.*

A day later we find Byrd writing a note to MacMillan, "stating that he will make another attempt to land gas at head of Flagler Bay, and, if possible, take a look into Canon Fiord, that is, if it meets with my approval. I wrote back that I would like to have him do it, but not to take any chances with clouds or fog."

On Aug. 16, MacMillan reported, the aviators succeeded in depositing a cache of food and gas in Sawyer Bay. Then a rumor (MacMillan, as always, had excellent sources in the Eskimo community) about Byrd's plans prompted MacMillan to place some limits on his activities.

AUG. 17: *I have learned tonight through Bromfield, the Eskimo interpreter, that he at the request of Byrd informed them that Byrd might fall over in Ellesmere Land, not on this next trip but on the one following, and remain there for the winter. He would like their help in sledging him on down to Upernivik in the spring. When the ice formed in Smith Sound this fall, he would like for them to come after him. He has learned* *that the house as built by the Canadian North West Police is habitable and well stocked with food, and that he will be very comfortable there. Knowing that was purely a publicity stunt, I issued the order that no plane is to fly without notifying me of its objective. I refused his request tonight to fly in one plane to Ellesmere Land, considering that two planes are out of commission....*

MacMillan was not alone in thinking it was time to head for home. In his journal he notes that the three staff members of the National Geographic Society on the expedition radioed their headquarters on Aug. 18, "urging the Society to order us to leave for home at once in order to give them the opportunity to do their work en route."

A day later, MacMillan himself decided it was time to head home. "I sent a letter to Byrd to discontinue all operations," he writes. On Aug. 21, the Secretary of the Navy sent a message (presumably via short wave this time) declaring "further attempts to fly over Polar Sea not advisable this season" and ordering its aviators to "withdraw with MacMillan and make such flights in secondary explorations as expedition returns south as you deem practicable after conferring with MacMillan. Department highly appreciates the fine spirit and splendid work of the Naval Unit under your command under very severe weather conditions."

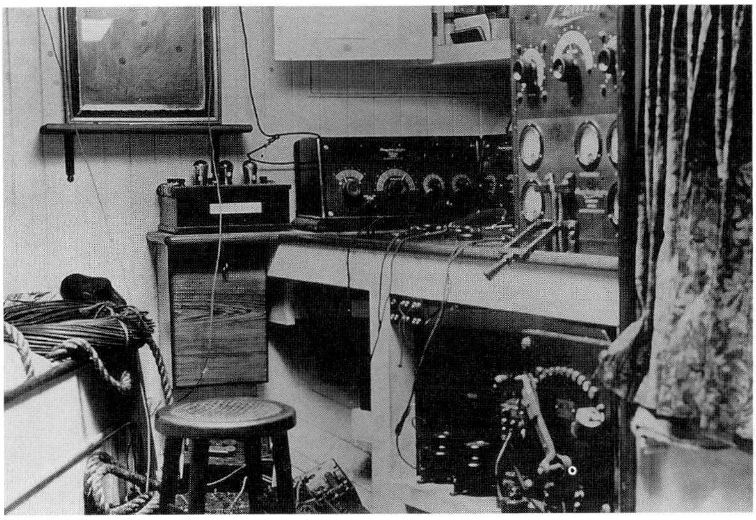

Shortwave equipment aboard the BOWDOIN.

The BOWDOIN, the PEARY, the Naval Arctic Unit and the rest of the expedition headed home, arriving back in Maine three and a half months after it had left. The ice-free time at their outpost in northern Greenland had been a little more than three weeks.

BROADCASTS

Eugene F. McDonald of Zenith Radio participated in the 1925 expedition to demonstrate the usefulness of his company's short-wave radio equipment for polar exploration and worldwide communications. The Navy's misplaced generosity with its out-of-date "spark set" — and MacMillan's creative response to the Secretary when ordered to take it aboard — provided an easy first opportunity to demonstrate short wave's superiority.

"It was plainly evident," MacMillan wrote in a June entry in his journal, "that the U.S. Navy had not as yet been introduced to the 'short wave' as used by the boys of the North American Radio League, the headquarters of which are in Hartford, Connecticut."

... Furthermore [the captain of the Navy Destroyer] did not know that the schooner BOWDOIN *was the first to ever talk with the world far to the south, following the law passed by Congress compelling thousands of amateur radio operators, many of whom had devised their own "sets" to abandon their 180 metres. This law was passed to rid the air of "trouble makers." The boys, obeying orders, began to send on 20 meters, and to their surprise and to the surprise of all so-called "hams" they were soon talking around the world!*

As the expedition proceeded, MacMillan and McDonald followed up with a series of publicity-generating "broadcasts" from north of the Arctic Circle to the rest of the world.

JULY 11 [LABRADOR]: *Gene McDonald ... broadcasted Sam Bromfield [the Eskimo interpreter] tonight, playing the violin and talking. If it went through to the States as we saw and heard it, it should be sensational, for Sam is certainly a character. I spoke for a few minutes also to the people at home....*

JULY 18 [LABRADOR]: *We tried to broadcast at 9 o'clock to America. We could be heard in Hartford, Connecticut, but not distinctly.*

AUG. 12 [ETAH, NORTH GREENLAND]: *Broadcasted tonight to America: (1) accordion played by Bromfield and Jacob Gayer. (2) music of the Eskimo by myself. (3) general introduction and remarks by McDonald. (4) singing by various Eskimos, and the beating of the "Ki-lau-tee" or Eskimo drum.*

AUG. 17: *We talked by voice yesterday with a 15-year-old boy in Cedar Rapids, Iowa. He answered in code, stating that he had heard our voices and music distinctly, yet he mistook the "Star Spangled Banner" for "Home Sweet Home!"*

The PEARY *established a two-way communication with New Zealand last night.*

MEANINGS

"The MacMillan Arctic Expedition of 1925 has actually gained in historical importance over time," write John H. Bryant and Harold N. Cones, the authors of *Dangerous Crossings,* a book-length account of the expedition published last year. They list radio communications and aviation among its significant accomplishments, and they characterize the expedition as an important "changing of the guard" in polar exploration. It "marked the handoff from the seaborne, sledge-based, terribly isolated expeditions of Nansen, Greeley, Peary, Scott, and Shackleton to the airborne, machine-driven, communications-linked worlds of Byrd, Lindbergh, and eventually Neil Armstrong." MacMillan would make two dozen more trips to the Arctic during the coming 30 years, but the 1925 expedition was his last "in the national spotlight as an explorer involved in high technology 'firsts.' "

Donald MacMillan had been a teacher before he first went north with Robert Peary in 1908, and after the 1925 trip his career again headed in that direction. The expeditions of the 1940s and 50s aboard the BOWDOIN, for which he is fondly

Navy and civilian members of the 1925 expedition prior to their departure, including Donald MacMillan, Richard Byrd and Eugene McDonald.

remembered by many students and researchers who traveled with him, were centered on studies of communities, wildlife, botany, ornithology, the Earth's magnetic field — topics of more interest to naturalists and anthropologists than to high-tech pioneers.

In a curious way, MacMillan and his "modern" 1925 expedition exemplify a very old connection between New England and the Arctic. In recent times the Arctic has seemed "remote," says Susan Kaplan, the anthropologist who directs the Peary-MacMillan Arctic Museum at Bowdoin College. "But a long time ago, the view was probably different; when people traveled by boat, the economy linked New England to the north; so the view then was different."

MacMillan sailed north in a vessel that recalled the fishing schooners of Nova Scotia. Like a fisherman or a fur trader he knew the value of local contacts and languages; his knowledge of the uncharted rocks, unpredictable icebergs, shoals and "tickles" of Labrador and Greenland was legendary. The Arctic, to him, was a place one sailed to, coped with, related to, learned from and then (one hoped) returned home from, safely.

The radios and airplanes he carried north in 1925 would change all that. Both the Arctic and the Antarctic became the focus of "big science" and technological exploits, such as Byrd's flights in the late 1920s and early1930s over the North and South Poles. The historic connections forged by fishermen, whalers, traders and dogsled-borne explorers receded in importance for a time.

Today, 76 years after MacMillan's pioneering trip, perceptions of the Arctic and its importance to the rest of the world appear to be changing once again. The self-sufficient native communities MacMillan took the trouble to understand are again providing models for understanding what constitutes small-scale community success.

"People continue to think of the Arctic as distant, remote, never changing, and that goes for cultures as well," observes Susan Kaplan. "They are surprised ... that people [in the Arctic] have automobiles and VCRs; they don't want to see that the Arctic is in fact quite relevant to them, whether it's because of whales, waterfowl, climate change. There are countless examples that the Arctic is linked globally; we've tracked pollutants from Pennsylvania to the Arctic, there are ramifications for global climate change."

Kaplan and colleagues at several institutions have been considering the "commonalities" among communities in the entire North Atlantic rim. "The North Atlantic is the most difficult part of the world to make a living, yet people live here," she says. "Are there commonalities, ways, cultures that have been successful?"

The answer, she believes, is yes — "Societies are small in scale. They have histories of doing a variety of things [to earn a living]. Their social structures are particularly keyed to being small societies that provide certain safety nets," such as kinship.

Donald MacMillan explored and pondered many of these same questions on his numerous trips to the Arctic. On the 1925 expedition, because he did many things well at the same time, he also provided a critical platform for scientific and technological innovation. In so doing, he made an enduring contribution to our understanding of the Earth's polar regions and their peoples, and of the connections between the Arctic and the rest of the planet.

***David D. Platt** is Editor of Island Journal.*

Two sources were particularly important in the preparation of this article: MacMillan's handwritten journal, housed in Special Collections at Hawthorne-Longfellow Library, Bowdoin College; and Dangerous Crossings: The First Modern Polar Expedition, 1925, *by John H. Bryant and Harold N. Cones (Naval Institute Press, 2000).*

Under the Line

For both Patriots and Tories in the Penobscot region, the American Revolution meant great suffering

RANDY PURINTON

When the British occupied Castine in June 1779, they believed that if they lost the war with the colonists, the new American country would extend no further east than Penobscot Bay. In their minds and in the minds of their Tory allies, lands eastward to the St. Croix River and into Canada would remain British.

They even reserved a name for the new region: New Ireland. It was as if they had drawn a line on the map, beginning at Bucksport and descending the lower Penobscot River, skirting Belfast to the west and Castine to the east as it passed over Islesboro and down the bay. It arced westward over Rockland and Thomaston, extended in the direction of Matinicus and then faded into the Gulf of Maine.

Illustrations by Robert Shetterly

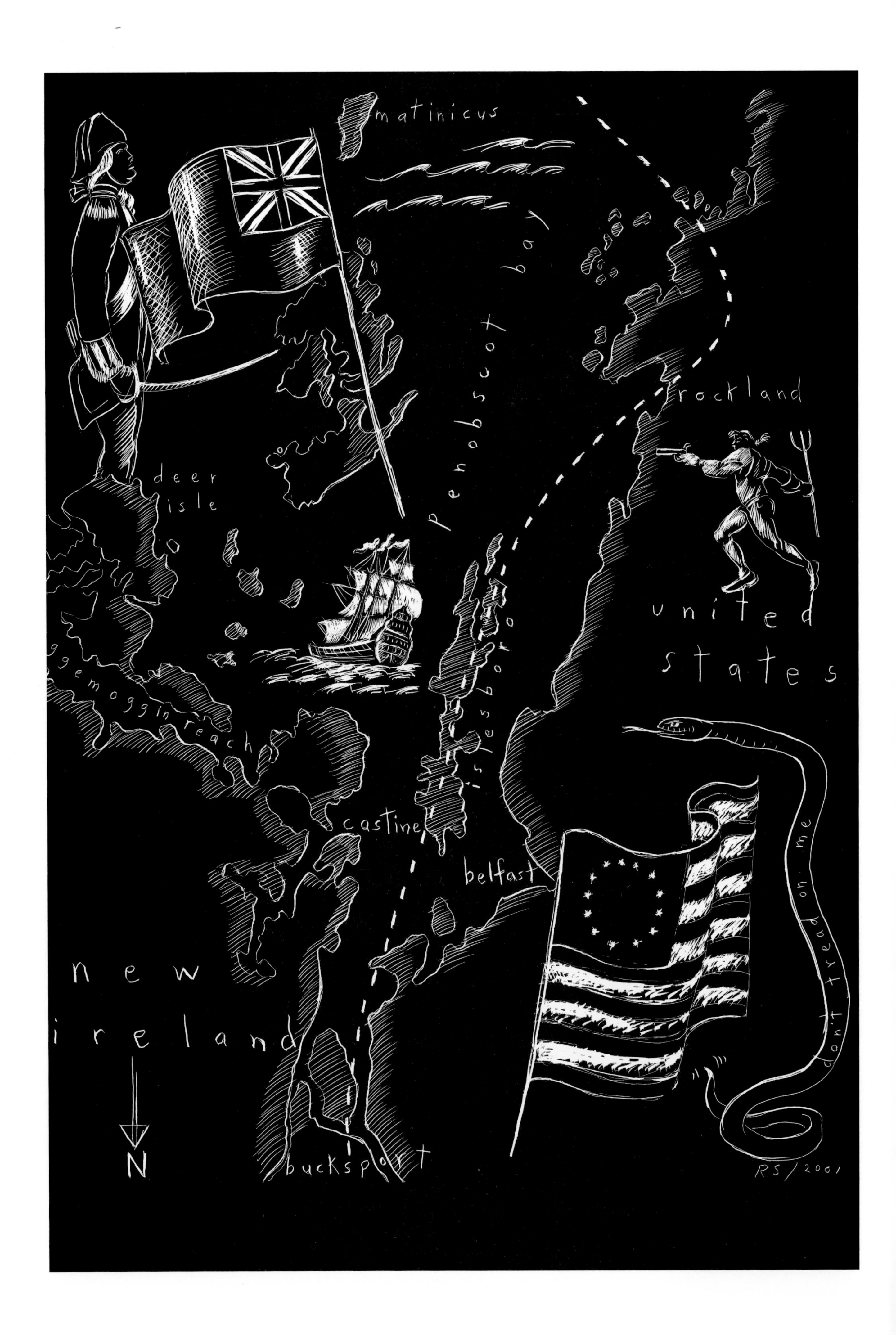
matinicus
penobscot bay
rockland
deer isle
united states
ggemoggin reach
islesboro
castine
belfast
new ireland
N
bucksport
don't tread on me
RS/2001

The line represented a hostile front between Americans and their British adversaries, and it set the stage for confrontations that provoked bitter memories. People who lived near and under the line suffered the worst.

Two British men, a naval captain and a civilian Tory were among those who shaped attitudes and aggravated relationships within a triad consisting of the British military based in Castine, the Tories who sought refuge and protection there, and settlers who were either patriots or desperately trying to persuade the British that they were neutral so they wouldn't draw attention to themselves.

Capt. Henry Mowat led the defense of Castine against the numerically superior American fleet that came to extract the British from its fortified harbor in the summer of 1779. He was a seasoned veteran of the King's navy, a professional who had a reputation among the patriots as a cruel bully but able adversary. He had been responsible for the bombardment and destruction of Falmouth (now Portland) in October of 1775. Though despised by his American enemies, few would deny that he was probably the bravest officer in either force during the siege of Castine. The ALBANY was his ship and one of the three that Mowat used to defend the harbor.

Dr. John Calef, a surgeon and chaplain of the garrison at Castine, was a Tory civilian who moved from Ipswich, Massachusetts, to Castine to advise Tory refugees and to further his interest in creating New Ireland as a commercially viable and permanent haven for loyalists. Because he was a popular and highly visible member of Castine's loyalist community, his perceptions of those who didn't share his views carried weight. He considered among his friends those in the local population who had sworn allegiance to the King by taking the Oath of Fidelity. In a letter to George III in 1780, Calef wrote, "the people of [this] territory have from the beginning of the Rebellion proved themselves firmly attached to your Majesty's Government, and several of them took the Oath of Fidelity to your Majesty in April 1779, and when Gen. McLean arrived at Penobscot with your Majesty's forces in June following, many hundreds of them took the Oath."

Those who did not take the oath became the objects of Calef's scorn: "there are upwards of Sixteen Thousand Souls within said territory," Calef wrote, "destitute of Law and Gospel, and having lived so long without either, and population increasing with amazing rapidity; their Children are growing up as Ignorant as the Heathen who dwell among them."

People who settled in the Penobscot Bay area were indeed living on the margins of American society geographically, but Calef seemed intent on marginalizing their very humanity because they did not share his political beliefs and his vision for New Ireland.

Living Under the Line

Immediately after the American defeat at Castine, life became tougher for people who lived under the line. It began at Bucksport.

The siege of Castine ended when the American fleet made all deliberate speed up the Penobscot River, with hardly a shot fired in the direction of the British naval reinforcements who had the wind and tides to their advantage. In the days following the rout, the British army at Castine ventured forth to pursue the remnant of the American forces. Because of Bucksport's proximity to Castine, and because Bucksport was in the direction of the retreat, settlers of that town fell victim to British plundering and burning. The house and vessel of Jonathan Buck, his sawmill and two barns were burned, and so were the homes of five others in the area.

Capt. Mowat was relentless. He sailed up the Penobscot to inspect the American wounded who were being removed to Boston under an agreement between Gen. McLean, commander of the British forces, and Col. Brewster, an American who lived on the river near Bucksport and who outfitted a ship for the mission. Mowat drew his sword against Brewster when he suspected the colonel of protecting a wounded American navy captain whom Mowat wanted to press into service in the King's navy. Mowat restrained himself, but it became increasingly difficult to guess whom the British considered their friends.

In his role as adviser and advocate for loyalists, Dr. Calef wrote to the King asking relief for three Castine families who were in jail for desertion and whose property was at risk of being confiscated. Dr. Calef explained that John and Joseph Perkins and John Hatch did not deserve their present state of confinement and deprivation. They were among those who invited the British to occupy Castine and, years earlier, they even sent lumber and supplies to the British Gen. Gage, when he and many loyalists were bottled up in Boston. Their actions had angered local patriots who, in a raid led by a Col. Cargill, seized their vessels and cattle.

The three men had given provisions and substantial help to the British during the early days of the occupation of Castine. But after the rout, these same men and their families became targets of insults, harassment and scorn from British soldiers, and they left Castine and returned to York. There, they were told to join the American military or be hanged. They returned to Castine only to be told that their leaving had been construed as desertion, so they were imprisoned. Only by signing over title to all their property would they be released. This they refused to do, and so they were "driven to a state of Extreme poverty and want."

•

Supporting one side or the other in the war could not guarantee one's safety. Trying to appear neutral was futile.

The British were firmly in control of Castine, but they knew they were not in control of the coast of Maine. To the east, the people of Machias proved that they could repel and frustrate the British. To the southwest, the headquarters of the American military in the region was based in Thomaston and led by Gen. Peleg Wadsworth, a capable and respected officer whose reputation was not tainted by the chaotic retreat from Castine. Though Wadsworth's resources were limited, he minimized the amount of food that the region's residents were selling to the garrison, thereby making life difficult for the British and their allies. Their efforts to feed themselves while at the same time maintaining their authority caused hardships and privations among those who lived near the line, most notably in the coastal town of Belfast.

The first settlers of Belfast had come in 1770 and 1771 when the area was still a wilderness. Food was caught in the sea, hunted in the woods, grown on rough farms. Cattle, oxen and sheep were brought. Hay was harvested. Clothes were handmade from wool. There was a sawmill. The settlers were poor, but not destitute.

Belfast was incorporated in 1773. In 1775 the war began, disrupting coastal trade. For a while, the port of Boston was closed. The demand for lumber declined. Gunpowder was in short supply and the threat of hunger was persistent. New settlers did not come and population growth stalled. In June 1779, the British occupied Castine, and Belfast began a slide into confusion and abandonment.

•

People who swore the oath of loyalty were promised permission to fish without being molested. Those who persecuted them for having sworn the oath would be punished. The King would guarantee the loyalists' property rights. Those who chose not to take the oath, it was implied, were vulnerable to molestation, persecution and seizure of their property. A majority of families in Belfast felt compelled to take the oath.

When the American fleet arrived, Gen. Lovell, commander of the expedition, issued his own proclamation advising the same people who had sworn to the King a month earlier to come to his camp and undo the damage by swearing allegiance to the United States. Otherwise, they would be considered traitors. Feeling reasonably sure that the Americans would prevail, Belfast residents went to Gen. Lovell, forsook their oath to the King and swore allegiance to the United States.

They would suffer for having crossed the line. Within a couple of weeks the flames of the burning American fleet were easily visible to the people of Belfast and it wasn't long before desperate American soldiers passed through their town, certain the British were on their heels. Having sworn away their allegiance to the King and joined the losing side, the people of Belfast knew that it was only a matter of hours or days before the British would exact a penalty. So the 18 families of the town buried the things they cherished or couldn't carry and abandoned Belfast altogether, moving as far as they could from the line.

In a town petition to the Massachusetts Senate in 1784, it was written that the refugees were "fain to seek their way through the wilderness to Settlements far enough out of the enemy's reach, they lived as Pilgrims in various places and enduring distresses painfull to relate but more Painfull to bear."

During the year or so that Belfast was deserted the town was plundered and houses burned by Tories. Of all the towns that lay near the line, Belfast suffered the worst.

Islesboro and the Line

With his family, Shubael Williams had settled on a couple of hundred acres in the area of Islesboro called the Narrows, an isthmus that divides the northern half of the island from the southern half. It was Williams's bad luck that the line that symbolized the hostile front between warring sides also ran through his property.

Islesboro's town history states that Williams moved to the island from Stonington, Connecticut, near the Rhode Island border. A husband and father of three, he was at one point pressed into service in the King's navy. He was probably wary of the British presence in Castine but not wary enough to hide from or avoid them.

Dr. Calef wrote that Williams frequently sold fresh food to the British troops, the kind of cooperation between civilians and the British that the American Gen. Wadsworth was trying to suppress from his headquarters in Thomaston. It would appear that Williams was trying to appear politically neutral but his effort did not protect him from being abused.

It seems that Williams was arrested by the British military for the crime of encouraging a British sailor to desert or for giving comfort to a soldier who deserted. The Islesboro history says that a sailor named Jackson was missing from a man-of-war at Castine. Williams was accused of aiding his desertion in some way. One account of the story says that a drunken sailor persuaded Williams to help him desert. Later, during testimony, this same sailor swore that Williams encouraged him to desert.

On February 10, 1780, Capt. Mowat wrote a letter to the commanding officer at Machias, an American patriot named John Allen. In this letter he accuses Americans of taking a ship's carpenter named Johnson off of one of the British naval vessels in Castine. Mowat demands that Johnson be returned immediately, in the same generous spirit that an officer of his had released some men captured at sea earlier in the year. In his reply, Allen denies knowing anything about Americans being captured at sea and then released. One can speculate that the "Johnson" of

Mowat's letter is the "Jackson" of Islesboro's town history. Perhaps Williams was one of the men captured at sea and used as a scapegoat to avenge the crime of aiding a deserter.

According to Dr. Calef, Williams was flogged in the summer of 1781. Other accounts date Williams's flogging to the summer of 1780. (If Williams was flogged in the summer of 1780 it would have happened sometime between the mysterious "Dark Day" of April 19 and the solar eclipse of October 27, as if the heavens conspired to reserve an inauspicious time for Williams's suffering, made worse by Williams's proximity under the line.) In any event it is known that Williams was arrested, taken to the British fort at Castine, court-martialed and sentenced to be flogged 500 lashes.

Flogging, or whipping, was not an uncommon punishment in Britain and America during this time.

One William Hutchings recalled that when he was a boy he saw two floggings on Mowat's ship the ALBANY. He also recalled a British soldier who was court-martialed and found guilty of desertion and sentenced to 200 lashes. "The blood ran down and filled his shoes," said Hutchings. The soldier was released after 100 lashes, probably because it became clear that he would perish if he suffered the full punishment and, after all, he was not sentenced to die. Williams's punishment, though brutal by our standards, was typical for his time.

Since flogging, like hanging, was designed both to punish and to deter, it had to be a public spectacle. The whip was a cat-o-nine tails, a bundle of nine leather cords attached to a handle, with nine knots tied in each cord. If the prisoner were sentenced to 500 lashes, as Williams was, he would actually be whipped around fifty-five times.

If the prisoner were a soldier, the flogging would have occurred during roll call and the posting of orders later in the afternoon, because the entire company would be assembled at that time and could witness and learn from the punishment. Because Williams was a civilian, it was necessary to gather local people to watch. "The neighboring inhabitants were ordered to be Spectators of the punishment," Dr. Calef wrote. Williams's punishment was supposed to deter civilians from encouraging soldiers to desert. Before the flogging of a soldier, a fife and drum marched before the assembly playing "The Rogue's March." If the same tune was played before Williams's flogging, it would have added to the humiliation of the prisoner while giving the musicians something to do that afternoon.

The whipping post was approximately six to seven feet high and it stood in the center of the fort's parade ground. Two iron staples — much larger than what we call a staple today — were driven into the post. One was about a foot below the top of the post. The prisoner's wrists were tied to this one; during the ordeal the prisoner's hands were above his head. The ankles were tied to the other staple that was near the ground. Sometimes, a man would be intentionally lashed so tightly to the top staple that in order to relieve the pain of the cords against his wrists he had to stand on his toes. As the flogging progressed the prisoner would become so exhausted that he could no longer do that. Then he just hung from the top staple, receiving the blows, groaning and bleeding profusely. The Islesboro history says that after 40 strokes with the cat-o-nine tails, Williams was released because 15 more would have killed him.

Though it's practically certain that Mowat supervised floggings aboard the ALBANY, it's less certain that the man who bombarded Falmouth and defended Castine witnessed the flogging of Shubael Williams. But he was in the area, knew about it and would have approved of it. Dr. Calef, who reported the flogging in his letter to the King entitled "The State of the District of Penobscot," most likely witnessed Williams's suffering. He observed later that the flogging had the appropriate deterrent effect because "many of the Old Settlers have left their possessions fearing the like treatment."

"Shaving Mills" and Patriot Plundering

Tory families fared no better, suffering persecution and plundering from the patriot side. John Carleton, a staunch loyalist of Woolwich, was confronted in the forest by a band of patriots called Sons of Liberty. They threatened to bury him alive unless he signed a certain paper that presumably demanded that he recant his loyalty to the King. He refused and began digging his own grave. The Sons of Liberty were so impressed by his tenacity that they let him go, but later plundered his house. Carleton abandoned his home and, with his wife and ten children, crossed the line to find refuge from persecution at Castine. Over time, it became increasingly difficult for the British to provide for the influx of loyalists.

While the British controlled Castine, their Tory allies scoured the islands in Penobscot Bay for food to feed their refugee families. Bands of marauding Tories sailed in small ships, tenders or whaleboats called "shaving mills." It's anyone's guess how these craft received their name, but the aftermath of their arrival in an area brought grinding poverty to the homesteads they raided and plundered. There were innumerable raids of this type on all of the inhabited islands in the bay during the war. Islesboro was regularly victimized by the shaving mills because of its proximity to British Castine. The homestead of John and Sylvina Gilkey of Islesboro suffered from one of these raids.

The story goes that while John was away a shaving mill landed near his home. The crew disembarked, drove the family's cows to the beach and shot them so they could be butchered on the spot. Sylvina shot at the Tories, who shot back at her, to no effect. She confronted them at the beach and tried to soften their hearts by telling them the difficulties and hunger her family would suffer if they took all five of the cows. The Tories left her one carcass, hacked the others into pieces of a size convenient enough to store in the shaving mill, and sailed back to Castine.

The shaving mills ranged as far as Matinicus. Joshua Thorndike, once a prisoner on the ALBANY for nine months, maintained a herd of cattle and a flock of sheep on the island for his father. Six months after he had settled there, Tories came in their shaving mill, shot the sheep, butchered the cows for transport and ransacked Thorndike's house. He abandoned the island.

The British were in possession of Castine until December 1783, when they were forced to leave by the terms of the peace treaty. Tory families left the harbor town to resettle in St. Andrews, New Brunswick, near the mouth of the St. Croix River. Williams's wounds healed, and he and John Gilkey signed the petition to the General Court in 1788 asking that Islesboro be incorporated into a town. The line faded into history.

Shubael Williams is described as an honest and practical man. He was the first in town to have glass windows. He built a kiln and made lime. It was noted in the town history, published 75 years after Williams's death, that the mortar made from that lime was still good and solid after all that time. He was a man who suffered and prevailed. His mettle was measured in the mortar he made, and on his back was etched the record of a life lived under the line.

Randy Purinton *writes frequently for Island Institute publications.*

MIRRORS OF INNER LIVES

Islands have inspired, challenged and instructed two generations of Wyeths

Those who study the psyche believe that anatomy is destiny; those who study nature believe that geography is destiny. Andrew Wyeth and his son, Jamie Wyeth, have immersed themselves in the nature of Maine islands since their earliest days, but have drawn very different kinds of inspiration from their island experiences.

Andrew Wyeth was introduced to the islands off Port Clyde by his best boyhood friend, Walt Anderson, a fisherman, a wanderer, and an explorer of the dark sides of life on islands and elsewhere. Andrew Wyeth's early watercolors drew their wild power and beauty from island landscapes and the chaos of their wave-wracked shores. These early watercolors helped catapult him to national prominence at his first one-man show in New York when he was 20. Andrew's early paintings of the Teels of Teel Island in Muscongus Bay, who had occupied this small family island since the early 19th century, in a sense presaged his more successful and well-known paintings of the Olson family of Cushing. These paintings occupied much of the middle of his career until Christina's death in 1968.

It wasn't until Andrew's wife, Betsy, bought Southern Island in 1978 that islands again regained a centrality in Andrew's paintings. Between 1978 and 1989, many of Andrew's best Maine watercolors, dry brush and tempera paintings reflect his life with Betsy on the 22-acre island. Situated at the entrance to Tenants Harbor, Southern slopes gently up to a prominent headland adorned with a gleaming, simple lighthouse that looks out over the western approaches to Penobscot Bay. For almost a decade, Andrew and Betsy spent summers in Southern's lightkeeper's house that Betsy carefully restored. Andrew did watercolors in a studio in the converted bell tower that once housed the harbor's fog signal.

Although Andrew, as always, painted constantly, he was restive. He felt trapped by Southern Island's size, and perhaps by its near perfection as an archetypal Wyeth backdrop. *Doctor Syn* (1981), which Andrew described as a self portrait, shows his desiccated skeleton sitting by a ship's cannon protruding from an open port in the bell tower. Occasionally he and Walt Anderson or other friends would steal off together, but Andrew's artistic preoccupations included escaping into the Helga series that he had been secretly working on as an antidote to the snug arrangements of the rest of his life.

In 1979 Betsy bought Allen Island, a 450-acre behemoth four miles off Port Clyde. Nearly the size of Monhegan, Allen had a few fishermen's shacks at its north end, but most of it was a wild and unruly place that Betsy tried slowly to pacify during the next ten years. She cleared the northern 40 acres of Allen to restore its pasture and brought in a flock of Metinic Island sheep. She barged off pulpwood and brought out a portable sawmill and well-drilling equipment. She built a barn and year-round residence. She built a road to the south end, dug four ponds and restored the oldest house on the island. And with help from local fishermen and their families, she began raising salmon in pens in the harbor and later blue mussels on rafts. Walt Anderson referred to all of this as "Betsy's Folly," and Andrew seemed assiduously to avoid Allen Island, lest he fall into another of Betsy's carefully constructed traps.

Long before, Jamie had immersed himself in the year-round island life of Monhegan, 12 miles out to sea. In 1967 Jamie bought the Rockwell Kent house, jutting out like a sharp jaw from Monhegan's southwest promontory, and he often used island friends as models for his work. He painted *Newt of Monhegan* (1986), and *The Islanders* and other island characters. *Breakfast at Sea* (1984) perhaps best captures Jamie's sense of the simultaneous dreamy beauty and desperate tension inherent to his view of island life. In the early 1990s Jamie began painting Orca Bates, who had grown up in the tumbledown house of Ray Phillips, the hermit on nearby Manana Island. Jamie captured Orca as a half-wild island child poised on the cliffy edges of manhood. But Jamie's fame and the increasing accessibility of Monhegan as a tourist destination began to impinge on his artistic freedom. He was reduced to working in a large wooden bait box when he wanted to paint a landscape, in order to avoid passers-by who would literally crowd over his shoulder to watch.

The twin pressures of Andrew's restiveness and Jamie's shrinking sense of privacy wore away at Betsy's island realm on Southern. Andrew perhaps facetiously badgered Betsy to dispose of Southern, and at dinner one night in 1990 she announced to her astonished husband that she had done just that. In a Solomon-like solution to her husband's and son's mirror image island dilemmas, Betsy gave Southern to Jamie.

Jamie moved out to Southern the next year and immediately flourished. The setting was perfect — just a quarter of a mile from shore — and Jamie could use this scant distance as a moat, and his outboard as a drawbridge, in order to work in the new castle of his imagination. A stream of stunning portraits (*Light Station,* 1992; *Southern Island,* 1994), island scenes (*Meteor Shower,* 1993), and landscapes (*Iris at Sea,* 1995) rolled off his palette as new energy from the island infused his work and output.

Throughout the 1990s Betsy spent nearly every day of her Maine life on Allen, and then later on Benner Island across the harbor, which she bought in 1989. By 1997, she moved from the mainland out to Benner lock, stock and barrel, and only left to cross the harbor to spend time on Allen. But Andrew usually only spent nights with Betsy at Benner, preferring to roam his mainland haunts and paint ashore in his father's studio in Port Clyde, Eight Bells. It was as if the architecturally austere compound of house, boathouse, chart room and barn that Betsy had created on Benner had become Andrew's newest Elba — as he frequently referred to it.

Nevertheless, Andrew could not expunge Betsy's islands from his imagination. Many of Andrew's most powerful Maine works of the 1990s, such as *Jupiter,* are set in the almost eerie quiet of Allen or Benner as violent tempests rage

Andrew Wyeth, *Pentecost*, 1989

around them. Andrew perfected his sense of almost violent alienation from Benner in *Airborne*, where the tattered flight feathers of a herring gull eddy in the wind as the curling white lips of foam gleam mercilessly from the island's edge. Images of conflict are rarely far beneath the surface of Andrew's work.

Always fascinated by the savage appetites of island gulls, Jamie began a series of paintings of ravens on Southern. Unlike the summer, when ravens are mostly solitary, in winter they gather in large flocks to forage for carrion. From Maine naturalist Berndt Heinrich, who demonstrated how ravens use complex calls to cooperate in feeding strategies, Jamie learned how to lure ravens to the shores of Southern. In paintings, he captured their hoary wildness in winter.

Perhaps Jamie's removal to Southern Island allowed him to view Monhegan in a new light. Free to come and go as he pleases, Jamie has begun returning to Monhegan mostly in the off-season. There his fervid imagination is continually fueled by the wild outer nature of gulls and ravens and the even wilder inner essence of his neighbors.

Maine islands have been at the center of Maine art for over a century and a half, and have gained a prominent place in American art partly as a result of their importance to the work of two generations of Wyeths. Of course, no two artists look at any subject in the same way, but rarely have two great American artists traveled over such similar landscapes and recorded such different moods. Andrew's island paintings are elegiac on the surface, but they are often dark and violent underneath. When Jamie's island paintings are dark, they are right-in-your-face dark, but with a calm sense of the strange and wonderful lives that lie within us beneath the surface. Perhaps it should be no surprise to discover that what artists find on islands is the mirror of their inner lives.

— Philip W. Conkling

Betsy Wyeth:
"I broke away and created my own world"

"It may be of interest to you to know why islands mean so much to me," wrote Betsy Wyeth to Philip Conkling after he shared the preceding essay with her.

"After over 40 years of strictly adhering to the Wyeth rule that only a location where one grew up was worthy of deep significance, I broke away and created my own world on my islands. It was a serious threat to A.W. and still is. Beats having a secret lover!"

"I know I've always been considered shallow within the Wyeth family for walking away, at age 18, from my upstate New York background and beginning life in Chadd's Ford. Cushing was accepted because that's where I spent my childhood summers. I even took a huge chance when I restored a mill property a mile from Chadd's Ford. I've been very careful to never travel abroad."

"With tongue in cheek I named the swank new boat I gave A.W. for his birthday HOMERUN *because (1) it goes like hell and (2) he uses it to come to Allen/Benner to spend weekends. The rest of the week is spent at Cushing and '8 Bells.' "*

"Two last things. Andrew's most famous painting is Christina's World *— done in Cushing! And his most popular recent painting is* Jupiter *— done on Benner Island! I gave Broad Cove Farm in Cushing to Nicholas. When I gave Jamie Southern, it was and always will be my favorite island. Both Southern and Broad Cove Farm mean everything to my sons. No strings."*

Andrew Wyeth, *Airborne*, 1996

Andrew Wyeth, *Bird Bath*, 1994

Andrew Wyeth, *Hand Lines*, 1997

Andrew Wyeth, *Scuba*, 1994

Andrew Wyeth, *Crew Neck*, 1992

Andrew Wyeth, *Jupiter,* 1994

Andrew Wyeth, *Embers*, 2000

Jamie Wyeth, *Tide Pool*, 2000

Jamie Wyeth, *The Island's School Teacher*, 2000

Jamie Wyeth, ***Sophomore at Bowdoin College*****, 1996**

Jamie Wyeth, ***Dead Cat Museum*****, 1999**

Jamie Wyeth, *Urchin*, 1999

Jamie Wyeth, *Ice Storm*, 1998

Jamie Wyeth, ***Lighthouse Tomatoes*****, 1996**

Jamie Wyeth, ***Whaling on Monhegan*****, 2000**

Jamie Wyeth, ***The Wind*****, 1999**

Gary Comer (3)

Free Willy – eat or be eaten?

COLIN WOODARD

A cold wind whips across the cliff-bounded bay on the island of Heimaey, Iceland, which is now covered in whitecaps. But Keiko the whale could care less. Circling in his enormous floating pen, the 10,000-pound star of the 1993 film *Free Willy* ignores wind, waves and even the puffins and fulmers soaring overhead. His attention is focused on the bright orange boat that has just tied up alongside the pen. On every lap around the soccer-field sized pen, he pops his head high out of the water to check out his latest visitors, looking very much like an excitable dog welcoming his human family home at the end of the day.

"Please, just try to ignore him," one of his trainers asks. "He recognizes everyone by sight and can get very excited when somebody new shows up."

At close quarters it's not an easy thing to ignore a 22-foot orca whale, particularly a trained one like Keiko. I'm promptly escorted to one of the floating pen's equipment shelters, which has an open door facing the gregarious whale. We remain in the shadows, where I am supposed to concentrate on interviewing the whale's trainers. It's hard to keep a straight face while standing there, dictaphone in hand, "ignoring" the whale. Every 30 seconds or so Keiko comes around for another pass just a few feet behind me, letting out thunderous exhalations as he lifts his head out of the water to peek inside the shelter.

But his guardians, the Santa Barbara-based environmental group Ocean Futures, have asked me to give Keiko the cold shoulder. They're trying to fulfill a promise to "Free Willy," reintroducing the orca to the Icelandic waters where he was caught

more than two decades ago. But Keiko was only two years old when he was taken from the wild. He's 23 today, and those intervening decades have been spent performing, entertaining and depending on humans. His trainers are trying to weaken his obvious bonds with people and encourage him to exercise, hunt and eat native fish, and explore the undersea environment.

But right now he's more interested in socializing with the media.

Occasionally I glance back and meet Keiko's curious stare and can't help feeling like I'm in the presence of a very big, very friendly, very intelligent family dog.

"You can't help but get a feeling of connection when you're with a whale," Charles Vinick, Ocean Futures' executive vice president, is saying. "They are thinking in some clear way. You get into the water with them and you say that there's a special connection going on that's almost physically tangible."

"They're very special animals," adds research director Jeff Foster, who's spent much of his life working with captive whales. He says orcas combine feline aloofness with at least canine intelligence. I'm wondering how the family dog would fare if returned to the wild. All the dogs I've ever owned would be begging at somebody's doorstep within a day or two. Will an orca be any different?

During this March 2000 visit, the trainers are busy trying to interest Keiko in chasing the live cod they've been releasing into his pen. They have large plastic tubs full of live cod, hovering in some confusion in the middle of their restrictive plastic ponds, perhaps sensing the adjacent whale through some gaddian sixth

Before a worldwide moratorium went into effect 11 years ago, 90-ton fin whales were harpooned, lashed to the side of the ship, and hauled individually or in pairs back to Iceland's single whaling plant in Hafnarfjordur.

While Americans are spending millions to rehabilitate a single whale, the Icelandic government has been threatening that it will leave the International Whaling Commission and resume commercial whaling.

sense. The cod were purchased daily from licensed fishermen here on Heimaey, the largest of Iceland's rugged and remote Westmann Islands. Before cod, Keiko was hand-fed high-grade frozen fish at considerable expense. Keiko eats about 100 kilos (260 pounds) of fish every day.

But food is just the tip of a dorsal fin when it comes to reintroducing a movie star whale to the wild. After starring in *Free Willy*, Keiko was discovered languishing in a poorly run Mexico City aquarium. The public outcry led a number of entrepreneurs to pledge to free the whale for real. Keiko was flown to Oregon, where he spent months in rehabilitation. In September 1998 he was flown to Heimaey in a specially modified C-17, which itself suffered $1.5 million in damage to its landing gear. He now has a full-time staff of 12 who fly in and out of Iceland to tend to his needs in a massive fenced-in bay, where equipment is often damaged by storms. Ocean Futures has spent about $14 million on the project to date, and continues to lay out $1 million a year.

Blasting and pile driving in the harbor, for a construction project to renovate the ferry slip that connects the island to Iceland proper, began in April. Whenever this is scheduled to occur, Willy is taken out on "walks" to avoid damage to his ears and internal sonar system. But when the weather makes it impossible to leave the harbor, Ocean Ventures has agreed to pay $6,000 per day for the construction crews not to work.

Keiko has been standoffish in his encounters with pods of wild orcas on his ocean "walks." Project staff admit it's entirely possible Keiko won't adapt to life in the wild, but they're going to give him at least another summer to make the proverbial jump to freedom.

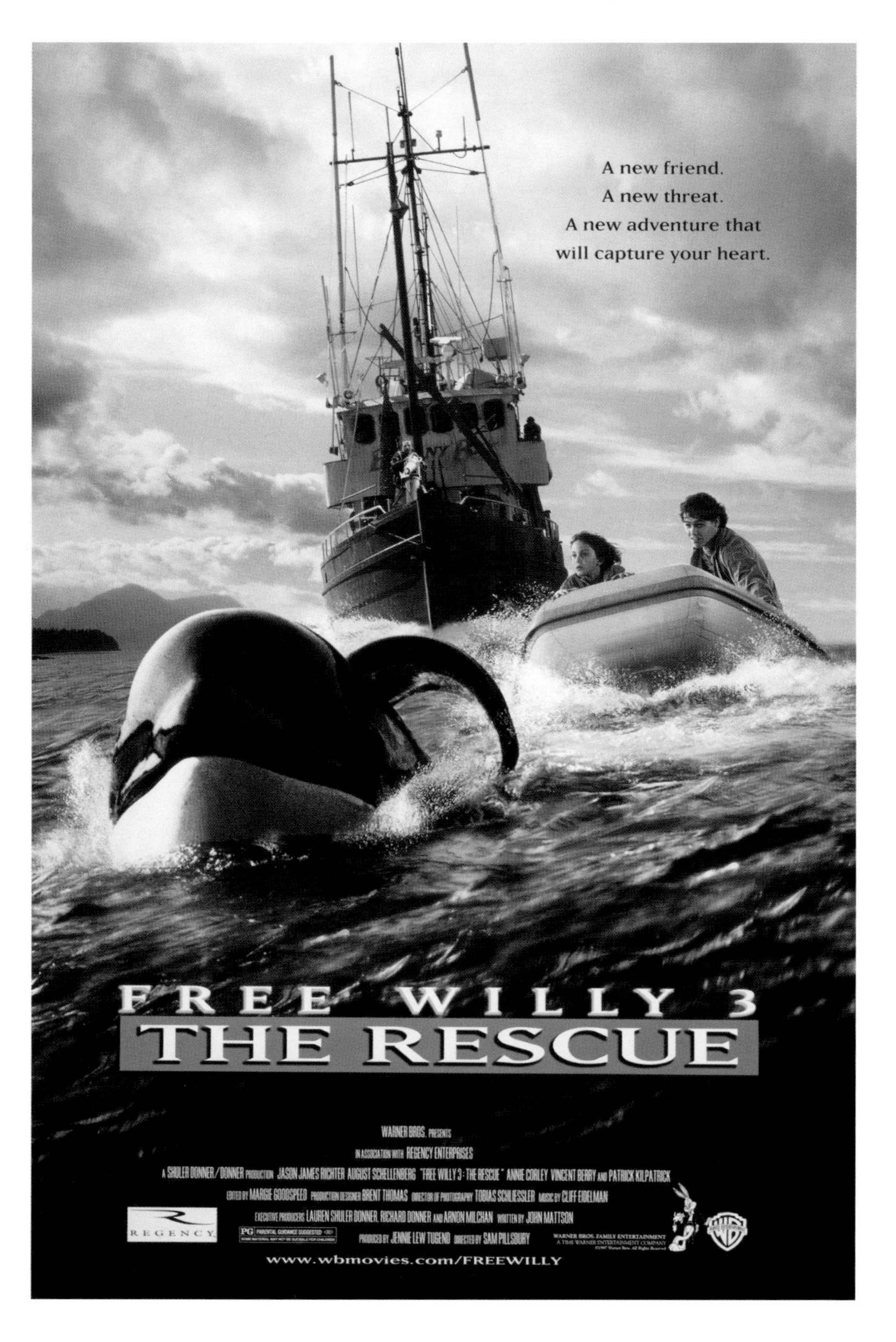

The transition from trained movie star to wild creature can be problematic.

The whole undertaking perplexes many Icelanders. Here humpback, sei, fin and minke whales have been hunted for centuries and are cherished not as individuals, but for their lean red steaks. While Americans are spending millions to rehabilitate a single whale, the Icelandic government has been threatening that it will leave the International Whaling Commission (IWET) and resume commercial whaling. Polls show these policies have the support of more than three-quarters of Iceland's 270,000 people.

"Whales are a renewable resource that we want to manage and harvest in a sustainable manner," says Johann Sigurjonsson, a whale fishery scientist and director of the Marine Research Institute in Reykjavik. "We don't accept that some animals in the ecosystem are holier than others."

This is the fundamental philosophical divide between whaling and non-whaling nations. The arguments are often cloaked in conservation rhetoric, framed in terms of whether sustainable whale hunting is possible for a given place or species, or if hunters use a particular technique. But the real difference, rarely spoken, is over whether a given species of whale should be hunted at all.

Many people in the United States and other countries believe

Charles Vinick, Ocean Futures

the great whales simply shouldn't be hunted at all. Whales — by dint of their magnificent size, appreciable intelligence and noticeable sociability — are regarded as fundamentally different from codfish. Keiko, the most famous nonfictional whale in human history, is the subject of considerable public interest, with tens of thousands following his progress on the Internet. Every piece of Ocean Futures merchandise, every press release and business card, features two names, side-by-side, beneath the logo: organization president Jean-Michel Cousteau and Keiko. Keiko, like many whales, has been inducted into humanity.

Most Icelanders don't see it that way. Whales are an exploitable natural resource like cod or herring, and their stocks should be carefully managed and sustainably harvested. Iceland even has an impressive record when it comes to fisheries management. Iceland fought several near-wars with Britain to protect its fisheries by creating the world's first 200-mile Exclusive Economic Zone. Canada and the United States fished their cod stocks into near-oblivion, while Iceland's cod fishing industry remains relatively healthy due to careful scientific monitoring and strict quotas.

Iceland even has an impressive record when it comes to fisheries management.

Sigurjonsson points out that based on the latest surveys, populations of fin, minke and sei whales are sufficiently healthy to sustain an annual catch of 100-200 of each. "Today I don't think [the anti-whaling argument] has anything to do with environmental conservation," he says. Based on the figures, Iceland's parliament has voted to resume whaling, but the government is moving slowly on the issue for fear of a boycott by major trading partners.

Iceland's four-ship whaling fleet has been tied up at a pier in Reykjavik harbor since 1989, when the International Whaling Commission's worldwide moratorium went into effect. For 11 years, Kristjan Loftsson has kept them heated and maintained, waiting for the ban to be lifted.

The day before I flew to the Westmann Islands, Loftsson, man-

Keiko's pen in Westmannaeyjar harbor on the island of Heimaey, Iceland. The whale was flown here from Oregon in September, 1998.

aging director of the whaling firm Hvalur, warmly invited me to tour the mothballed fleet. From the flying bridge of one of the 600-ton whaling ships, he described how 90-ton fin whales were harpooned, lashed to the side of the ship, and hauled individually or in pairs back to Iceland's single whaling plant in Hafnarfjordur. The trip took 18 hours each way, which imposed a sort of structural limitation on the whale fishery. At the plant the meat and blubber were frozen for human consumption and the vast majority exported to Japan, where it commands a high price as sashimi. The bones and offal were processed for oils or pet food. "Nothing was wasted," he says.

Loftsson, a gracious and friendly man with a full beard and smile, proudly showed me the ship's quiet, steam-driven engines, its massive boilers, and how to load its three-foot long exploding harpoons with black powder. The whales died instantly, he says, and large pumps kept cold seawater running through their bodies to keep the meat as fresh as possible. The ships were built in Norway to hunt whales in the Antarctic and tow them to much larger factory ships that processed them at sea. Hvalur purchased the catcher vessels after commercial extinction of many whales made southern ocean whaling unprofitable.

"The history of whaling is not something I can vouch for," he says. "The great over-harvesting in the Southern Ocean during the 20th century was terrible and should never be repeated. But Iceland didn't take part in that. We're being punished for mistakes others made 70 years ago."

Iceland — along with the U.S., Canada and other countries, played a part in hunting many North Atlantic whales to commercial extinction. The parliament banned whaling from 1915 to 1948, the year Iceland became fully independent from Denmark. After that the industry consisted of Hvalur's single plant and four small ships, which typically processed 240 fin, 70 sei and 80 sperm whales a year.

"It's political nonsense that's all," Loftsson says of the IWC's moratorium. He doesn't buy arguments that whales are

Keiko swims beneath the surface on an ocean "walk" as Ocean Futures staff members monitor his behavior.

Keiko's teeth are checked daily as part of his routine health care.

Ocean Futures (3)

Three spots under Keiko's chin are visible during a "spy hop." Such markings make it possible to identify individual animals.

exceptionally intelligent or critically endangered. "They are animals like any others. To apply human intelligence criteria to them is absolute nonsense.... If the stocks can sustain the harvest, we should utilize them."

As for Keiko he only shakes his head. The project will fail, he predicts, because Keiko is "a sick whale." He worries that the Hollywood star may carry Pacific pathogens to North Atlantic whales, thereby endangering the orca stock. But ultimately, he says, "I could care less about the animal."

The Hvalur fleet may one day return to hunting fin and humpback whales off the west coast of Iceland. That's because the IWC ban was put into place to give stocks time to recover and thus to ensure the future of commercial whaling. As populations of some whale species grow, so does pressure to remove the ban.

Environmental groups opposed to whaling — Loftsson calls them "the crazies" — still do so based on protecting the stocks, rather than risking what would probably be a losing moral argument. "As an organization that has branches in many different countries including most of the Arctic countries we try to stay clear of saying that any animal is a special animal," explains Cassandra Phillips, the Worldwide Fund for Nature's (WWF) U.K.-based whaling coordinator.

"Certainly for a lot of individuals, myself included of course, we feel a special sort of resonance with whales. They're absolutely fascinating and it's very exciting when you see them. But it's probably not enough of an argument to say that none of them should be hunted."

WWF is lobbying the member states of the IWC hard to prevent a resumption of commercial whaling by Japan and Norway, fearing that lax monitoring, underreported catches and considerable profit incentives will decimate many whale species that have only just started to recover from the abuses of the past two centuries. It supports very limited whaling by native people, but regards commercial, export-oriented whaling operations as a slippery slope back to the bad old days.

Colin Woodard (3)

Top: *The Hvalur whaling fleet may one day return to hunting fin and humpback whales off the west coast of Iceland, but for now, its rusting ships are berthed in Reykjavik harbor.*
Bottom: *Krisjan Loftsson*

But the conflict over the moratorium is tearing the IWC apart, raising concerns that it will collapse, triggering a whaling free-for-all that could decimate many whale stocks.

Norway resumed commercial hunting of minke whales in 1993, defying the IWC moratorium. It has increased its quota every year since then and plans to kill 753 of the 25-foot long whales this season. Norwegians eat much of their whale meat, but hundreds of tons of blubber are collecting in freezers unused.

In the 1999-2000 season, Japan's distant-water whaling fleet killed 389 minke whales for "scientific purposes" inside Antarctica's Southern Ocean Sanctuary, causing a diplomatic uproar.

Nobody hunts orcas for food, so Keiko's prospects in the wild will largely be determined by Keiko and his trainers.

When we left the floating pen, the wind was starting to stiffen. Waves exploded into spray on the 27-year-old lava flows that form the other side of the island's harbor. Twin volcanic cones loomed; above the sea — one created centuries ago and covered in grass, the other, a heap of steaming red gravel, was created in 1973. The ocean beyond looked harsh and forbidding, a place where ice and lava flows sometimes meet in crunching, hissing collisions. I wondered what Keiko made of it — if he thinks about such matters at all — whether he'd prefer life out there to his carefree captivity in a U.S. aquarium.

As we powered our way across the harbor, I asked Jeff Foster what would happen if Keiko decides he prefers captivity to the chilly waters of southern Iceland. "We're not taking any chances with Keiko's life," he said. "If need be, we're prepared to take care of him for the rest of his natural life."

In September, 2000, Ocean Ventures announced that the two-year effort to reintroduce Keiko to the wild had failed and they would return him to a captive life – ed.

Colin Woodard *is author of* Ocean's End: Travels Through Endangered Seas *(Basic Books, 2000).*

IN THE PINK

A researcher learns just what (and how much) herring gulls eat

WING GOODALE

The hydraulic winch whirrs and resonates with the thundering diesel engine, a symphony led by the VHF radio and mewing gulls. Herring and great black-backed gulls call frantically as Jessie Lermond helps her father check the first lobster trap of the day. Scott Lermond, a member of a Rockport fishing family, pulls out the lobsters, replaces the bait, points out a pink gull, and yanks crabs off the green mesh. I confirm the sighting and mark a GPS position. I watch intently as Jessie tosses the rotten herring overboard. The pink undersides of the gulls' wings flash as the birds dive at the sinking bait, snatching it from the water with a ruckus of calls and squabbles.

During the past two summers, these pink herring gulls became a familiar sight in western Penobscot Bay as unsuspecting participants in my research. For three years as a graduate student at College of the Atlantic, I looked for the answer to one question: how important is lobster bait to gulls?

Pink dye encircles a clutch of herring gull eggs, ready to mark the hatching chicks.

Opposite page: Gulls of another color: an undyed herring gull soars over others that have been dyed pink for the author's experiment.

I asked because lobster bait may be providing gulls with a majority of their food during the breeding season, May through August, when food availability may well determine the number of gulls that live along the coast. High gull numbers are a problem because the birds seem to be winning a race for survival. They are out-competing smaller seabirds, their numbers remaining high while colonies of terns, puffins and other smaller seabirds survive on just a handful of islands.

My interest in gulls and lobsterboats was sparked during the summer of 1998 when I had the opportunity to protect terns by working for the U.S. Fish and Wildlife Service. As I assisted with the first stage of restoring a tern colony on Metinic, non-lethally removing gulls, I found myself shooting off flares and disturbing gull nests. I soon realized that this wasn't completely effective, possibly because the gulls were receiving ample food from nearby lobsterboats: the food subsidy of discarded lobster bait outweighed the deterrent of flares.

Why do gull numbers increase while terns do not? It's a matter of lifestyle — terns prefer fresh fish, while gulls are omnivorous scavengers. Because humans have provided ample scavenging opportunities, from open dumps and chicken farms to fish factories and fishing discards, the gulls have thrived. In fact, a 1960s herring gull study in Penobscot Bay found that more than half of the birds' diet came from human sources.

Because dumps, chicken farms and fish factories have either closed or been cleaned up, the gulls' food subsidy today is limited to one source: discarded lobster bait. Lobstermen fish up to 800 traps, which they set in lines of 10 to 15 pairs called strings. Depending on the season, they haul each string every three to ten days. Once the trap is on board, lobstermen keep the legal lobsters and put in a bag of new bait. They toss the old macerated bait overboard since it no longer attracts lobsters — much of the bait has been eaten by other marine organisms and on what is left the herring oil has washed away. Although the bait may no longer be useful to the lobstermen, it still provides a high calorie meal for gulls.

The behavior of gulls flocking around lobsterboats may have its roots in an ancient commensalism — one species benefiting from another without harming the host. Gulls depend on lobsterboats as they do whales. Studies have shown that the birds will seek out whales, alight near them, and wait for fish escaping the lunge-feeding cetaceans. In the same manner they seek out vessels, alight near them, and await the bait tossed from trap-hauling fishing boats. The hungry scavengers may have an innate tendency to feed on bait discards.

Wing Goodale (5)

Marked gulls enabled the author to track them as they moved among the islands, ledges and lobsterboats of Penobscot Bay.

PINK DYE

I wanted to learn firsthand just how important discarded lobster bait is to the scavengers. Do the birds fly a long distance to locate lobsterboats, or do they eat discarded bait only when it is conveniently dumped around their breeding colonies?

During the summer of 2000 I descended on Robinson Rock, a ledge in western Penobscot Bay, and dyed approximately one hundred of its gulls bright, indisputable pink. In this way I could track the gulls with GPS, knowing where they were from. I contemplated several marking techniques, but one was clearly the simplest: sprinkling dye powder on the nest.

When I actually approached the island I felt like I was in combat — surging surf and diving gulls, strong winds and jagged shoreline, uncertain footing and hip waders an inch too short. After a hair-raising landing, I staggered from nest to nest in seawater filled boots, sprinkling a fine powdered dye around the speckled eggs in the hopes of marking the gulls' feathers when they returned to incubate.

The next day I was thrilled to find healthy pink gulls exchanging glances. My pink subjects were generally unfazed; the real confusion came from bird watchers and unsuspecting lobstermen. One summer resident, John Macomber of North Haven, confided to me that he thought he'd seen a Ross's gull, a rare Arctic visitor with a pink belly. A North Haven lobstermen described the consternation of his sternman. "He says to me 'Jesus! Did you see a pink seagull?' I saw it, but I looked him straight in the eye and said 'I don't know what you're talkin' about.' " After I sent word to local newspapers, Al Gardner, a local cameraman, called to tell me he had filmed a pink gull on Tolman Pond . . . and it was going to be on the local cable station.

Combining my sightings with those of Penobscot Bay fishermen and residents, I found that, although a few gulls were flying as far as 18 miles for this bait subsidy, the average distance was closer to five miles. Interestingly, a majority of the sightings were south of the marking site, likely a result of the increased fishing effort in the southern part of the bay. Lincolnville, Islesboro, Camden and Rockport each have 30 to 35 lobstermen while Rockland and Owls Head have 155. The correlation between the number of lobstermen and the concentration of sightings suggests that gulls actively seek lobsterboats for food.

WELL-FED CHICKS

After discovering that gulls actively foraged for bait, I wanted to know how much bait they consumed. I decided to focus on the chicks, which adults gulls feed by regurgitating. Visiting gull colonies located north to south in Penobscot Bay, I collected diet samples from their chicks on Flat, Mouse, Goose and Ram islands, and on Robinson Rock.

Once again, my methodology seemed clear when I designed it in front of the fireplace, but I had overlooked my biggest foe: the ebbing tide. Jauntily, I beached my boat, tossed the anchor ashore, pushed the small craft into the water, and set off to collect diet samples — not giving a second thought to the falling tide. An hour later, I returned with a notebook full of data to find my boat ten feet from the water's edge. A blistering string of oaths and grunts helped me muscle the vessel over large boulders, off small ledges, and back to the water. Within two weeks my aluminum outboard resembled a colander. In fact, without flotation, it would have sunk. Midway through the season I had to sell my poor vessel for a hundred dollars, procure a replacement, and radically change my landing technique.

Back to the unfortunate study chicks. Much to the displeasure of the young gulls, I extracted diet samples by sticking my finger down their throats and pulling out their breakfast. Bait was easy to identify by its strong odor and pasty consistency. Luke Lermond, Richard's sternman and son, joined me one day and unequivocally agreed that what I called bait was bait, the same stuff, he pointed out, he spent all day pitching.

Sometimes the bait's odor was so strong I nearly produced my own regurgitates. I became desensitized to the smell, but my friends and family often turned away in disgust when I returned at the end of the day.

Not all the samples were bait — crabs, blueberries, marine worms and insects were common, as well as samples of picnic lunches including spaghetti, white bread, smoked chicken, sliced red onions, and of course French fries. But, when I tallied my samples, I discovered that half of what the gull chicks ate was discarded lobster bait. Not only is this bait consumed at all times of day, tide, and weeks, but rotten herring also appears to be consumed by the entire population. Since bait offers more calories per unit than any other food besides fresh fish, rotten herring may actually provide three-quarters of a chick's daily requirement. The contents of a quarter-full bait bag has enough calories to sustain a chick for a day.

"After a hair-raising landing I staggered from nest to nest in seawater filled boots, sprinkling a fine powdered dye around the speckled eggs."

Peter Ralston

Ten to 18 million pounds of lobster bait may be consumed annually by Maine gulls.

If the diet samples are broken down by island a pattern emerges: the percentage of bait increases in incremental steps from north to south — Flat, the most northerly island, only had 7 percent bait while Ram, the most southerly, had 50 percent. Like the pink gull sightings, the increase of bait in chick diet coincides with an increase in fishing effort, suggesting that the number of fishermen in an area can indicate the amount of bait being fed to the gull chicks.

A WHOLE LOT OF BAIT

I knew that Maine lobstermen used approximately two hundred million pounds of bait, but how much could the gulls actually get? Tackling this question meant hauling with lobstermen like Scott and Richard. Soliciting their help was the best way to gain an introduction to Penobscot Bay since the fishermen, acute observers of nature, helped me learn exactly how the gulls behaved.

One day while on board with Richard Lermond, I was able to observe firsthand how the birds acted around a boat from which bait was tossed overboard. Fieldbook in hand, I scribbled notes as Richard and Luke worked fluidly and efficiently. "Now watch!" Richard yelled over the din, "soon as the trap's half way up, the gulls will fly in." Sure enough, as the first trap surfaced pink and slate-colored herring gulls settled around the boat, while great black-backs waited on the sidelines. In contrast, when I went hauling with Bill Reidy from Islesboro, who kept his bait on board, I didn't see a gull all day. The gulls appeared to know which boats discarded bait and which kept it on board, congregating around the vessels that discarded before they had even left the harbor. Terns and other specialized feeders haven't a chance against such well-fed competitors.

As we worked from trap to trap, I recorded data and asked questions. I found that approximately three out of four fishermen toss used bait overboard. The others either dump the used bait in their trap, hoping it might still lure lobsters, or keep it onboard so that the pesky gulls won't be attracted. During the height of the season, traps are hauled approximately every four days with one quarter of the bait still in the bag. When the discards were tossed overboard, the birds recovered about half— the other half sank. In other words, ten to 18 million pounds of lobster bait may be consumed annually by Maine gulls.

I was unsuccessful at marking great black-backed gulls or collecting diet samples from them. However, I did observe that black-backs seem to recover less bait than their smaller cousins. Instead of diving at the sinking bait, they stole from herring gulls, probably because the black-backs are bigger and it's difficult for them to maneuver tightly for sinking bait. The black-backs' predatory habits may provide them with enough food from other sources, such as eider ducklings.

MANAGEMENT

Simply put, lobster bait is herring gulls' primary food source during the breeding season, a plentiful food source that gulls actively seek. Since food availability is the primary force supporting seabird populations, rotten herring may be supporting Maine's high herring gull numbers. A reduction in discarded lobster bait, therefore, might decrease gull populations. Numerous other studies support this supposition, demonstrating that when a food subsidy such as open dumps or fishing discards is removed, gull populations nearly always decline.

Since convincing an entire industry to reduce its bait discards would be a challenge, and since herring gulls pose the greatest threat to nesting populations of smaller seabirds like terns, a better plan might be to address discards only within a few miles of tern colonies. Fishermen in such areas could be asked to help keep old bait from gulls by discarding it into their traps where it sinks, or to keep it in a bucket onboard and discard it all at once at the end of the day. The fishermen's efforts would have to be complemented by seabird restoration teams harassing gulls around tern and puffin colonies. If the effort was successful, gull populations could decline, lobstermen could be relieved of the pestering gulls, and other seabird species could re-establish themselves.

During a foggy day at the end of July, Scott Lermond's BLACK LABEL emerges from the impenetrable whiteness as I navigate my boat home. I gun the engine and cut a wide circle around his vessel, slowing as I near the pilot house. "Have you seen any pink gulls," I yell over the din of the wind, gulls, VHF and two engines. "Nope, haven't seen one for a week now." I wave, bring my boat back up to a plane, and head towards Mark Island. Within moments Richard's blue hull appears in front of me with the obligatory gulls. I ease down to an idle and Richard turns to me. "Where's Luke?" I ask. "Oh, he's off fishing with his cousin today," he replies as he tosses a couple short lobsters overboard. He looks up at me with a broad smile and says, "Heard on the radio you were bothering the seagulls again."

"Yup, but I think that's my last visit for the season . . . all the chicks are off on their own. Best not keep you from your traps." He gives me a thumbs up as he throttles up and heads to his next string. The handful of white, freeloading gulls take off and melt into the fog with Richard.

Wing Goodale *described the early stages of his gull-and-bait research project in* Working Waterfront *in 1998.*

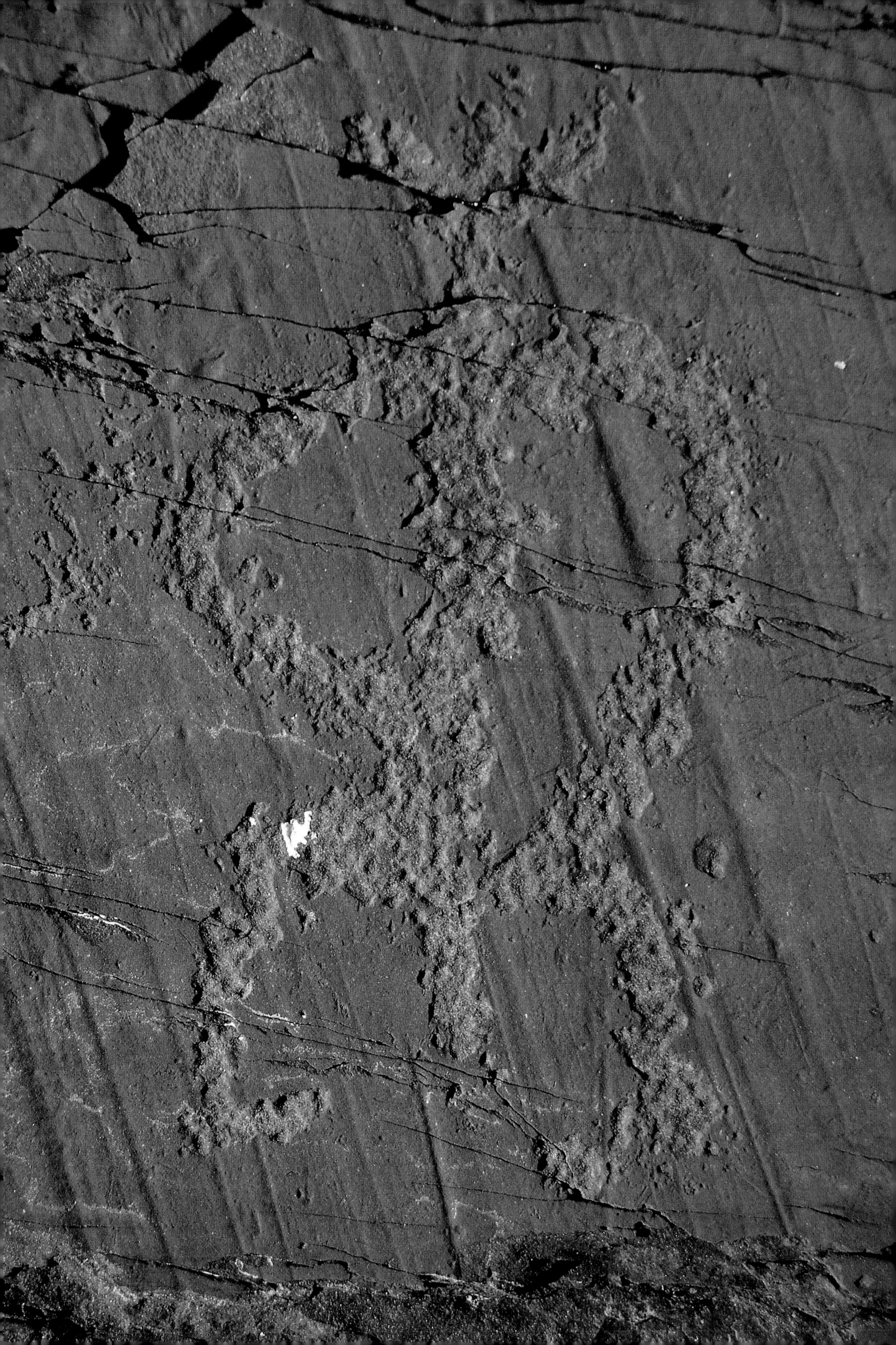

FROM DEEP TIME

What do Machias Bay's rock carvings tell us?

BONNIE L. MOWERY-OLDHAM

Rick Jordan (6)

Serpent petroglyph.

Imagine, if you will, two or three thousand years in the future, someone exploring the coast of Maine. Among the artifacts of past inhabitants, they find a crucifix. Turning this object in their hands, they wonder at its function and meaning. How can they possibly grasp this relic's religious significance, or the way this symbol helped a certain segment of humanity to connect with powers beyond themselves? Could its significance be truly understood? Such dilemmas often surround artifacts found outside the context in which they were created — they are cast adrift in time. Researchers must contend with similar factors when investigating Maine's bountiful trove of Native American petroglyphs — rock etchings with spiritual powers and ritualistic purposes.

Left: Petroglyph showing a messenger, replete with horns and tail.

A petroglyph thought to depict a Native American sweat lodge.

The term "petroglyph" means, literally, "marks on stone." The world's oldest rock engravings, etched some 45,000 years ago, are found in Australia. In Maine, petroglyph sites have been discovered along the Kennebec River in Embden, along Grand Lake Stream and in the Machias Bay region, where the largest concentration of Maine rock art occurs. Mark Hedden, archaeologist with the Maine Historic Preservation Commission, regards Maine's petroglyph sites as the most important on the Eastern Seaboard because of their numbers — Maine has the largest available collection of recorded rock art in the Northeast — and their age. Most of the carvings are 1,500 to 3,000 years old. Maine petroglyphs have a time-depth greater than any other examples of rock art east of the Mississippi River in North America.

The Machias Bay petroglyphs occur on extensive slate ledges that are rust or maroon-colored. The glyph maker, most likely a shaman, chipped the carving into the ledge using a hammer-stone of a material harder than the bedrock. As the thin volcanic ash coating was flaked away, the black slate below it showed through with enough contrast to create the image. The difference between the pecked design and the rock surface made the designs clearly visible and even today, centuries later, they are distinguishable from the rock bed. Archaeologists infer that native glyph makers would have been able to see previously made designs and avoid overlapping designs. Hedden believes that repeated visits by shaman practitioners occurred over periods of time, ranging from a generation or two at Grand Lake Stream, to many centuries at Embden, and millennia at Machias Bay.

The Machias Bay petroglyph sites are located within two miles of each other. They appear oriented in four directions, perhaps representing the shamanic circle of life — north (the spirit world), south (mid life), east (spring), and west (old age). The northern site includes petroglyphs of a caribou, a walrus, a sweat lodge, a row of dancers holding hands. The eastern site has primarily human-form figures of various designs, some measuring 14 feet tall with antlered headdresses. The western site has many petroglyphs of animals, and the southern site includes a mixture of both human-forms and animals.

Machias Bay seems to have been a major center of activity for indigenous people from early prehistoric times into the "contact period" when non-indigenous peoples ventured into the region. According to a 1993 *Island Journal* article by Maine Historic Preservation Commission archaeologist Arthur E. Spiess, there were few European traders venturing into the area during the 1500s, when most trading of European goods was conducted by Micmac traders who obtained trading items from Europeans in the St. Lawrence Gulf area. Between 1605, when Champlain mentions Maine ethnic groups, and 1676, when the Indian wars brought dramatic changes, three ethnic tribes inhabited Maine and the Canadian Maritime Provinces: the Souriquois, Etchemin, and Abenaki. The Etchemin are ancestors of the Maliseet and Passamaquoddy, the tribes who primarily journeyed to the Machias Bay area. The Etchemin were hunters, fishermen and gatherers of wild plants for food.

It has been hypothesized that a major epidemic, perhaps hepatitis, greatly reduced the size of the Passamaquoddy nation during the contact period. There is evidence, including Micmac-style petroglyph designs at a Machias Bay site, that some members of the Micmac tribe joined the Passamaquoddy tribe at that time, helping the nation to survive. Native American activity in the Machias Bay region persisted into the 1700s, and as late as 1790 an eyewitness account tells of seeing 100 Native American canoes pulled up to the shore at Holmes Point, while their occupants sang and danced until daybreak. Even as late as 1920, one finds oral references, from Maine sources, of shamanic gatherings.

The Machias Bay region was important to the Passamaquoddy because of the extensive clam flats along the Machias River estuary, the seasonal runs of both Atlantic salmon and alewives into the river, and the abundant supplies of lobster and fish from the ocean. Moose and game animals were plentiful, and an eel fishery was also established.

To European settlers, the Machias Bay region was considered a backwater. Hedden believes that the Algonquian-speaking people gathered in the autumn, when the likelihood of encounters with foreigners diminished, for their seasonal gatherings and ceremonies of power and healing.

According to Hedden, the carvings represent multiple layers of meaning that are difficult for non-Natives to grasp. Westerners' literate-based source of authority, stemming from writings and books, contrasts with Native Americans' source of authority, which is based on non-literate knowledge gained from shamanic visions and dreams. Since westerners' knowledge of Algonquian language and culture is limited, it's not surprising that their ability to interpret petroglyphs is similarly limited.

The Passamaquoddy nation, over 40 percent of whose people speak and understand their native language, has been experiencing a revival of interest in its traditional culture. There is reason to believe its members have some idea of the multiplicity of meanings these images represent. Even if they do, it seems unlikely they would actually share this information with anyone outside of the Native American family. Archaeologist James L. Swauger remembers Shawnee tribe member John Reese asking him, "Do you think we'd tell you the real name and power of a design? Sure, we'll tell you something to keep you happy, but we'd never tell you the truth. Power lies in the true knowing and revealing the truth would kill the power."

MYSTERIOUS FORCES

Machias Bay Boat Tours and Sea Kayaking, a touring enterprise run in the summer months by knowledgeable naturalists and Maine guides Martha and Rick Jordan, conducts visits to petroglyph sites. The Jordans believe that Maine's petroglyphs are a national treasure, having withstood the forces of time, tide and weather for hundreds of years. Respect for their significance and fragility tempers the Jordans' enthusiasm, and Rick has expended uncounted rolls of film documenting the glyphs in photographs such as the ones accompanying this article.

The petroglyph sites aren't easy to find. I wouldn't have been able to find even one of them were it not for the Jordans' guidance. Even at the northern site, looking directly at them, I might have overlooked the faint marks if the Jordans hadn't pointed them out. Clearly anticipating my somewhat let-down reaction, Captain Martha Jordan whipped off her sock, dabbed it in sea water, and lightly rubbed the petroglyph so the image would appear. I stepped back and squinted, and, as the images took shape, I experienced a sense of awe.

The Jordans pointed out image after image. There was a caribou, a walrus, a sweat lodge, a stickman holding a large halibut, a shaman brandishing his two turtle credentials, and intriguing, recurrent spirit figures, with their spindly multiple limbs suggesting an eerie etheriality.

As I viewed a line of figures holding hands, seeming to dance into the sky, I couldn't help but wonder what message they were meant to convey. Later, when I read Mark Hedden's comparison of mnemonic glyphs to "beads on a rosary string," I thought, yes, that's exactly what they are.

Bonnie L. Mowery-Oldham

Tour guides/petroglyph afficionados Rick and Martha Jordan.

The petroglyph sites are special, sacred places, sites to be respected and honored. While there, I could almost visualize the Native Americans who once inhabited the site, and could almost smell the sweetgrass used in their ceremonies. I felt a bit like an intruder viewing the ke-kee-no-win images, and I hoped that the reverence I felt would make my presence more acceptable to the mysterious forces that might still be hovering in the air and embedded in the rock.

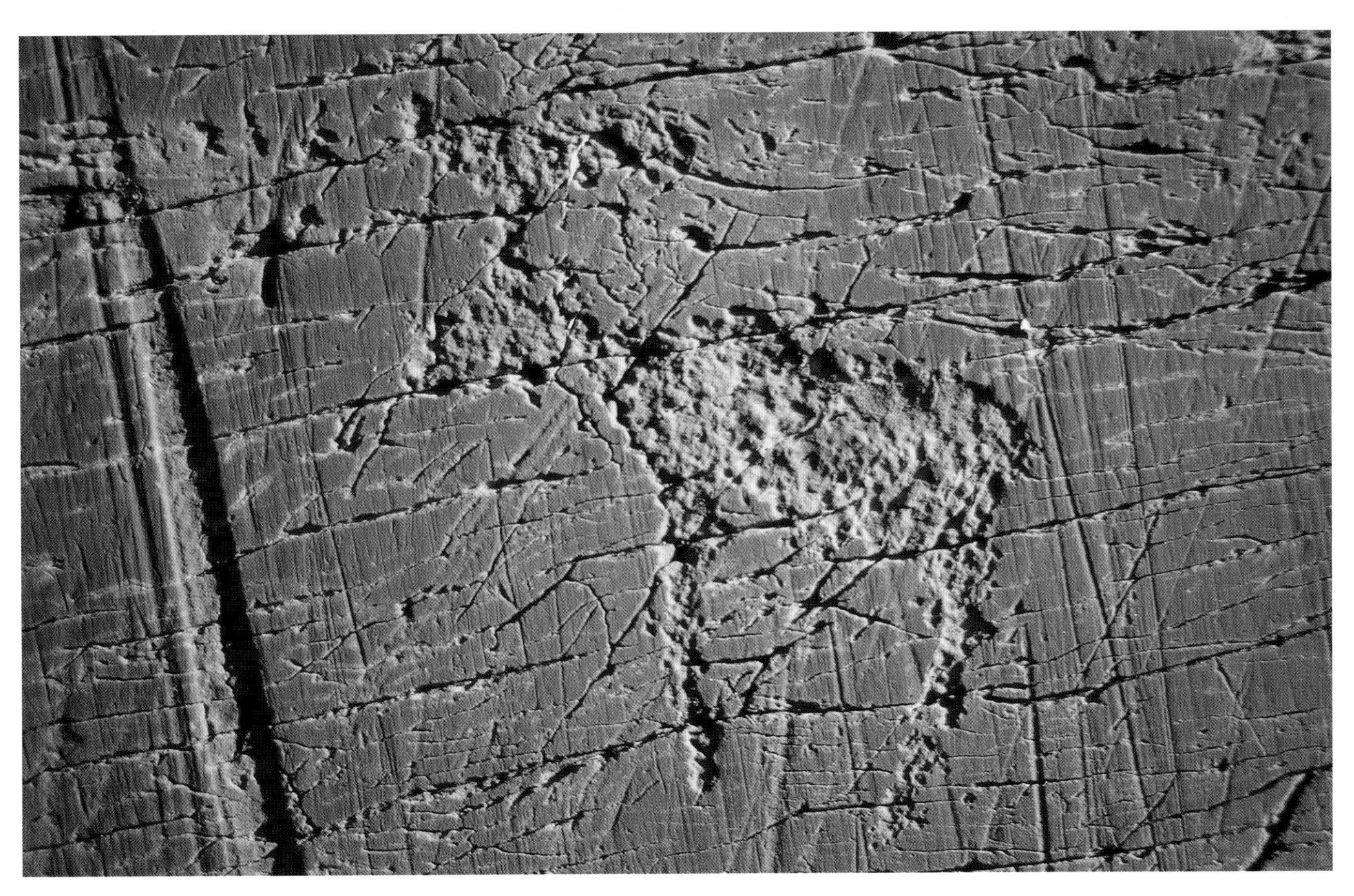

Leaping deer petroglyph.

Swauger also recalls that a Navajo soldier once told him with a smile that he and his friends loved anthropologists because "they write down anything we tell them."

Swauger has extensively researched the rock art of the eastern woodlands, a 14-state area ranging from Virginia to Maine. When he began his studies in 1974, he was confident that he could eventually find answers to all the questions that plague archaeologists. He discovered design similarities among various Maine petroglyphs and noted their substantial differences from rock art found in the southeastern United States. Yet after finding and studying 352 sites, he still can't say why a particular rock area was chosen as a site, except that carvers seemed to prefer sandstone to granite. The reason for carving the glyphs has continued to elude him. He wrote in 1993 that after nearly 20 years, he was as ignorant now as to "why men and/or women carved or painted designs on natural objects in the 14 northeastern states as I was on 5 June 1958 when I first visited the God Rock. Perhaps they were created as parts of rituals: secular, religious, magical. Perhaps they were created to record events, private or group: sad events, glad events, historical events. Perhaps they were territorial symbols denoting boundaries, trails, directions. Perhaps they were but aimless scratches and daubs of color."

Image of large antlered anthropomorph with bent elbows and three fingers.

The first mention in print of North American petroglyphs is to be found in Jesuit father Jacques Marquette's 1673 journal, where he wrote of winged monsters carved in rock in what is now Illinois. Garrick Mallery — author of *Picture Writing of the American Indian,* the first major book on North American rock art, which appeared late in the 19th century — noted that "one of the curious facts in connection with petroglyphs is the meager notice taken of them by explorers and even by residents other than the Indians, who are generally reticent concerning them."

Mallery personally visited the Machias Bay petroglyph site in 1888 and established two important facts about these petroglyphs. First, they were the work of Algonquian-speaking Native Americans, and second, the designs could not be "read" as a form of writing.

Left: Petroglyph merging attributes of spirit guide and shaman.

After Mallery's findings became public, many professionals lost interest in the "doodle bugs," dismissing them as mere scribblings and scratches. They did arouse some interest among local people, however: E.W. Moore of Embden photographed the Kennebec River ledge in 1894, and Edward Brown of Machiasport photographed a section of the Maine Ledge at Machias in 1922. Both of these photographers used chalk to highlight the designs.

Swauger, Hedden and other archaeologists strongly believe that the carvers of Maine petroglyphs were shamans. Swauger hypothesizes that they came from a peaceful people, because few weapons and no scenes of warfare are depicted at the sites. Most of the Machias Bay glyphs are spirit, or shamanic, images. There are animal shapes, mostly game and lizard-like creatures, and an abundance of hourglass shapes representing the anthropomorphic motif of spirit/shaman. One stylistic trait — the rectanguloid torso outline — is a distinctive early feature.

Thunderbirds, triangular torso anthropomorphs with birdlike features, are a common type of petroglyph found in Algonquian ideology and at Maine sites. These images are thought to represent shamans with special connections to the heavens, who could take spiritual flight to intercede for the people.

What westerners can study and comment on with certainty is the chronological progression of distinct types of petroglyph styles found at the Maine sites. In the spring 1991 Maine Archaeological Society Bulletin, Hedden asserts that "there is a remarkable consistency in the spread of the triangular-bodied stylistic convention throughout all the northern Algonquian speaking groups from Maine to Minnesota ... These distributions point to a continuing, though perhaps intermittent, exchange of ideas during a minimum of 1,500 years between Central and Eastern Algonquian shamans, despite physical separation."

Hedden initially became interested in prehistoric rock art in the 1950s while working at a Columbia River archaeological site, where his job was to explore and record findings before a proposed dam flooded the region. He discovered a huge selection of petroglyphs. There wasn't much archaeological interest at the time in studying these prehistoric lifeways, and Hedden volunteered many of his off-hours to record the rock art. As is often the case in archaeological fields of study, funding became haphazard, forcing Hedden to abandon the project. Hedden's interest in petroglyphs continued after he moved to Maine, and, starting in 1977, he began systematically recording the entire collection of Machias Bay and Kennebec River glyphs for the Maine State Museum. He used a variety of techniques including black and white photography, scale drawings and "surface printing" (recording imagery using cloth and paper). He also conducted field surveys for new sites, and developed a relative chronology of petroglyph design styles.

The well-documented rate and timing of sea-level rise over the past 5,000 years, resulting in glacial till erosion and ledge exposure, makes it possible to pinpoint fairly accurately the dates for the different styles of glyphs.

At a newly-discovered site in southern Machias Bay, Maine's archaeologists began a systematic examination and documentation of the rock carvings in May 2000. This is just one part of the long-term analysis of the Maine petroglyphs supported, in part, by the Maine State Museum, the Maine Historic Preservation Commission, and the Maine Archaeological Society. The results of the ongoing study have been published as an ongoing series of articles for the Maine Archaeological Society Bulletin between 1983 and 1991.

Neglect has been helpful to the preservation of North American petroglyphs, since the elements of mother nature are no match for the destruction that humans inflict. The Machias Bay glyphs have withstood time and tide, but the heavy foot traffic of tourists walking on sites and general sightseeing activities cause considerable damage. The glyphs are very fragile, and Hedden urges visitors to use extreme care while viewing them — don't walk on them, chalk them or even touch them. The Maine Historic Preservation Commission, along with the Maine tribes, would like to see these sites protected. There is speculation that the Passamaquoddy nation may take over wardenship, and, working with the state, map out a plan of site control and preservation.

Doodle bugs, scribblings, power images, teaching tools: what do they mean? Maine petroglyphs are as shrouded in mystery and meaning as a modern-day crucifix found along the shores of Machias Bay would be to future explorers. With all the questions that remain unanswered about prehistoric petroglyphs and Maine glyphs in particular, why should we study them? Why do we find ourselves intrigued and awed by them? Perhaps it is our need to work out the puzzle of the past's connection to the present. Perhaps, instinctively, we sense their still-lingering power. Or maybe it's because, as archaeologist James L. Swauger would have it, "the effort is sufficient justification for us to take to the hills and the forests to continue our fascination with these relics of the past."

***Bonnie L. Mowery-Oldham** contributes regularly to Island Institute publications.*

STORY IN STITCHES

A remarkable quilt recalls a method of fishing now gone by

MURIEL L. HENDRIX

"It was awful," says Ernie Burgess.

"It was always blowin,' Ray Hamilton adds, and Burgess agrees.

"You couldn't see anything," Hamilton says, and tells how early one morning he stepped in a bucket in the dark, got his foot caught and couldn't get it out. "About a year ago, I called up the guy who was on the boat with me then," he continues. "I hadn't talked to him in 30 years, but his first words were, 'You got your foot out of that bucket yet?' "

Burgess

Sitting in Ernie Burgess's kitchen on Chebeague Island, they are reminiscing about longline fishing, or trawling. They are among the handful of people still around who participated in this arduous way of life, which they learned from their fathers and grandparents. Beside them hangs a quilt Burgess's mother, Shirley Burgess, 82, created to preserve and commemorate this bygone method of fishing. Although Ernie Burgess and Hamilton describe it as awful, they have great fun remembering its character-building hardships, adventures and challenges. By comparison, lobster fishing, they agree, seems boring and repetitious.

In the early 1900s, as many as 35 Chebeague fishermen earned their living longline fishing. Today, none do. Longlining off the coast of Maine was pushed aside in the mid-70s after the federal government encouraged large fishing draggers and groundfish became depleted. Regulations got so stringent it no longer made sense to go out trawling. Shirley Burgess says that now, "A lot of native people whose ancestors, even their fathers, worked at longline commercial trawling don't know anything about it." Being a woman of considerable determination and energy, Burgess, who created the Maine Lighthouse quilt that hangs in the lobby of the Island Institute building in Rockland (*Island Journal,* 1995), decided to employ her talent as a quiltmaker to document the process of this bygone skill before it was lost altogether.

Groundfish swim across the top of Burgess's quilt, which is made of fabrics that in some places are painted with a special dye to intensify colors. The cod, haddock and cusk are padded a little and underpainted with an iridescent paint that adds a silvery sheen. Beneath are six pictures, which, like stained glass windows that relate Biblical stories, portray parts of the longlining process.

In the first panel a fisherman uses a six-tine pitchfork to toss mussels into the punt he has pulled up on a Chebeague beach. He works on a sunny day, at the edge of bright blue water, quite different from the dark gray and almost black waters of subsequent scenes that take place on the winter ocean in early morning and late afternoon.

Next, two fishermen work in the fish house, one of five once located on the beach shown on the lower, large panel. They bait the "trawls," a task that took about two days, and generally, as in the picture, attracted other men to socialize. Each trawl is a 3,000-foot, 14- pound hemp line. It has 500 hooks attached to the end of "gangion" lines that hang from the trawl at six-foot intervals. One man shucks mussels; the other baits the hooks.

Muriel Hendrix (2)

Ray Hamilton (left) and Ernie Burgess

"Now, people have never heard of baiting with mussels," Ernie Burgess says, "the el primo haddock bait. They don't know how to put one on a hook." (Herring, mackerel and squid were also used.)

"God, it was a lot of work," Burgess says to Hamilton, who nods assent. "Cold, too. I remember steam coming off people's hands while they were shelling mussels. Every once in awhile, you'd have to stick your hands in the stove door."

Unless the weather was poor, the men would bait 10 trawls, with each line coiled slightly off center in a wooden tub and the baited hooks arranged in the

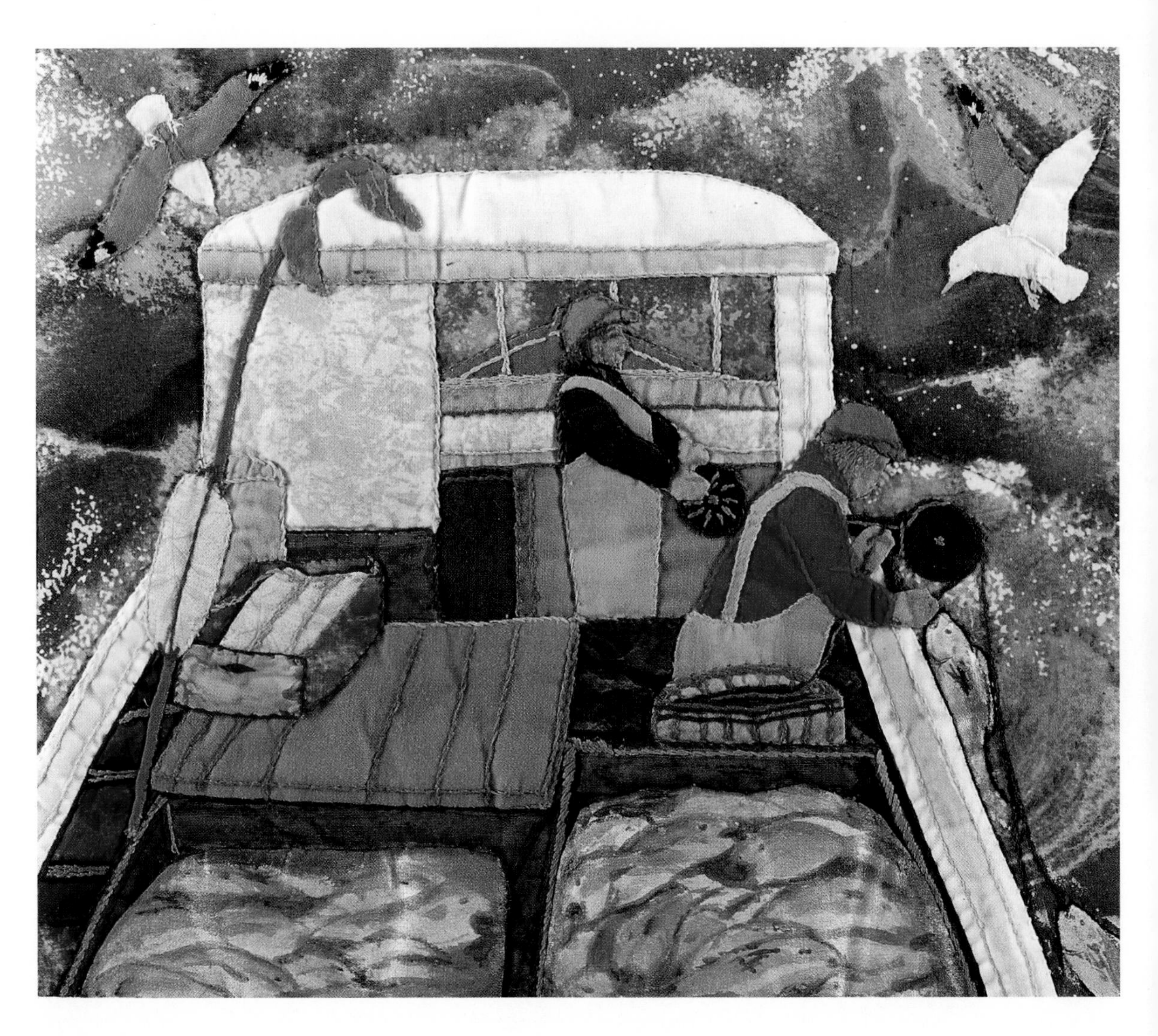

Above and opposite: Shirley Burgess adapted some of her quilt "squares" from photographs.

leftover crescent-shaped space. If the weather turned bad, the baited hooks would keep for a week or two, but after that, the men would have to knock the bait off and start over.

Fishermen sailed out to fishing grounds in the early days in schooners and then set out in dories, and later used 35- to 40-foot lobster boats. They usually left at midnight. This would give them time to reach fishing grounds by dawn, and then set and haul the lines by the following night. They navigated by dead reckoning. Ernie Burgess relates how over and over when he was a kid, he watched his grandfather steam towards Jeffreys Ledge, keeping the Portland lights lined up to determine his drift. "The old guys always knew where they were," he says. "My grandfather would slow down, get out the lead line to sound, and he'd say, 'We're gonna hit forty fathom,' and 99 out of 100 times we would."

The year Hamilton and Burgess fished together on Burgess's boat, Burgess set the trawls while Hamilton ran the boat and kept him supplied with tubs, as portrayed in the third section of the quilt. Once Burgess threw out the initial buoy, attached to the end of a trawl and the "ballicky rock" (a 30-pound weight that would take the trawl to the bottom), the trawl would start to fly out. "You dropped the rock over and then you'd set like hell," Burgess says. It was a tricky, dangerous business. Some fishermen were pulled over and drowned; others who were caught were more fortunate like one Hamilton recalls, who got the trawl line wrapped around his wrist. "He was alone," he says. "To save himself, he grabbed the staysail mast and hung on till the line parted."

Most men used a setting stick to flip the gangion lines free as the line flew out. When one trawl neared its end, another was quickly attached to make a continuous line with intermediate buoys to keep the trawl visible.

A ten-tub trawl, set in about an hour, would extend six to seven miles. Once it was set, the line would "soak" while the men steamed back to the beginning, grabbing some beans, franks and coffee on the way (they also might make a

chowder after they got some fish). They would then begin the arduous eight- to ten-hour haul, the subject of the quilt's fourth panel.

Cod ranged from 18 to 40 pounds; the larger ones were gaffed. Cod would swallow the hook deep, Burgess says; to dislodge it, the hauler would swing the smaller ones in an arc over his head and snap his wrist when they landed in the fish tray to make the hook straighten and release. It would be re-bent with a special tool during the next baiting session. "Haddock would spin on the hook and sometimes you'd lose them," Burgess added. "You had to pull them in gingerly because they have a soft mouth. Cusk would take in air and blow up; sometimes two or three tubs would be afloat." The fishermen never could be sure what might appear: Burgess's father, Alger, once caught a 300-pound halibut on a 6.0 haddock hook.

If the weather was good and sea relatively calm, the person handling the boat would gut fish during the haul, and the two men finished gutting during the four- to five-hour trip back to Portland. "There were guts and gulls and gull droppings everywhere," Burgess says. In a gale, they would run for Fort Gorges and hang out there while they gutted the catch, usually 5,000 to 6,000 pounds.

Often, they reached Portland Harbor close to midnight. Burgess and Hamilton remember nights when the ice was so thick they followed a pilot boat in or couldn't get through to the dock. Once there, as shown in the sixth panel, they pitched the fish into a twine or canvas basket so it could be hauled up and dumped on the wharf for culling. One of several receipts Hamilton saved shows that on May 2, 1944, cod brought six and one-half cents a pound, haddock seven cents, cusk five and one-half cents. The take was divided three ways: a share for each man and one for the boat. "It was a lot of work for the money you got," Burgess notes.

Shirley Burgess has donated the quilt to the Chebeague Historical Society, which will hang it in a museum being established on the island. There the quilt can teach today's and coming generations about this piece of island life, which would have been lost but for Burgess's effort.

Lee Bowman (2)

Muriel Hendrix *writes regularly for Island Institute publications.*

Fox Islanders Go Rowing

Students and their teachers build boats, community and character

BRUCE HALIBISKY

Students from both communities had to build shops before they could build boats.

On a Thursday morning in late summer, VIXEN, a 32-foot Cornish pilot gig with six oars and a crew of seven, weaves its way out of Carvers Harbor away from the island of Vinalhaven. Attempting to follow the stroke's lead, my hands pull at the loom of an 18-foot port side oar. At the helm, Gigi Baas grimaces into the fresh southerly breeze blowing up the harbor and maneuvers us around the paint-peeled skiffs and moored lobster boats.

"Port side hold water. Starboard side make way," she commands as we veer to avoid a mooring. Her body cranes as if trying to wish a bowling ball out of the gutter and we narrowly clear a barnacle-covered buoy. As we pass the docks, lobstermen look up from their work and give shouts of encouragement. We make our way out to the green can marking the entrance to the harbor, passing the herring boat STARLIGHT, rafted to the outer fuel float.

"Pull together, now," Gigi urges, shouting over the squawking seagulls that wheel and dive around STARLIGHT.

In this working harbor filled with lobsterboats and bait docks, VIXEN's long oars and bright red hull appear out of place — a summer folks' toy or maybe a mainlander's idea of recreation. The boat, however, is a product of the island, built by Vinalhaven School's Marine Technology class. It is actually the fourth school-built Cornish pilot gig to be launched into Penobscot Bay.

On this particular morning, VIXEN is being rowed by a group of women called the Granite Island Girls (G.I.G.) This rowing club encourages Vinalhaven women to get out on the water for exercise, companionship and the pleasure of rowing. The Granite Island Girls are one part of a larger group of islanders — including lobstermen, teachers and students — who regularly take VIXEN rowing in the waters surrounding Carvers Harbor.

As we turn into the stretch of water between Lanes Island and Vinalhaven, Gigi invites us to take a break and remove extra layers of clothing. Leaning against the hull of the boat, Gigi says, "Most kids out here have been fishing all their lives. They just wait to finish high school so they can get back to fishing. Building VIXEN, they learned some things that were in line with what they would do after school." Reflecting on her experience of rowing in VIXEN she continues, "I've been out here on Vinalhaven for 16 years and I've always seen the water as a barrier — something you had to cross on the ferry. VIXEN has allowed us to get out on the water for fun."

> ***Competence, Compassion, Challenge and Community***
>
> *—North Haven Community School motto*

In 1993, Ron Watson, the Marine Technology teacher at the Deer Isle-Stonington school, read about Cornish pilot gigs in an article in *WoodenBoat* magazine. The gig's design comes from Cornwall, England, where the boats were used to take pilots out to ships arriving from the Atlantic. The gigs are capable of making up to eight knots under oars and are known for their ability to go to sea in almost any weather. Traditionally built Cornish pilot gigs are now a competitive racing class in England.

Watson remembers someone at the school suggesting that he try to build a Cornish pilot gig with his students. At first he thought the idea was crazy but then, having heard about similar projects at the Hull Lifesaving Museum outside of Boston, he decided to take on the challenge.

Once a shop was constructed, the students built a fiberglass version of the Cornish gig. Then, using the first gig as a mold, Watson and his students built a second one. Hoping to create a fleet of boats that could compete against each other, Watson sent out letters to all the high schools with access to Penobscot Bay, encouraging them to build their own gigs. At the time there was little response to his proposal.

In 1997, however, a group of students at the North Haven Community School, working with their teacher John Dietter, decided that they wanted to build a boat as an elective class. Dietter had heard about the gigs in Stonington and realized what an ideal project building a boat would be for an island community. He sat down with the students and they tried to figure out what would be needed to construct a gig. The first item on their list was money. The students wrote grants, resulting in funding from the North Haven Arts Enrichment Foundation, the Island Institute and MBNA. John is quick to point out that the seven students who worked on the gig organized everything from balancing the checkbook to building a shop. Using the strip-planked method of construction, North Haven's gig was built with the help of boatbuilder Charlie Pingree and launched in May 2000.

Peter Ralston

Vinalhaven students and their instructor worked on VIXEN *through the winter.*

In Vinalhaven, the driving force behind building a Cornish pilot gig was the Vinalhaven School's Marine Technology teacher, Mark Jackson. When Jackson was hired in 1998 he was determined to focus on projects that would relate specifically to the students of this fishing-oriented community. In his first year of teaching, his students designed and built scale-model lobster boats. The second year Jackson wanted to try a project that would encourage teamwork as well as develop patience and craftsmanship. Inspired by the North Haven Community School and Deer Isle-Stonington projects, Jackson recruited six students to build a gig. After securing a grant of $9,388 from MBNA, lofting of the 32-foot boat began in the fall of 1999. The students worked through the winter and by the end of the school year, the gig, called VIXEN (playing with name of the Fox Islands) was launched into Carvers Harbor.

Billy Dickey, 18 years old, worked on VIXEN from start to finish during his senior year of high school. His summer after graduating has been spent mowing lawns and working at the island's lumberyard. After rowing with Gigi and the Granite Island Girls in the morning, I go up to the lumberyard to talk to him about building VIXEN. The sun is emerging through a layer of morning fog and Billy squints his eyes, his hand held up to his brow. As he talks he leans against a dumpster among the stacks of lumber and looks into the distance. From time to time he turns towards me for emphasis.

Throughout the project, Billy documented the building process with a camcorder. He has 15 hours of video and would like to take a course at the Maine Photographic Workshop in Rockport to edit all the footage into one concise tape.

Billy is proud that his town and school came together on the day the boat was launched. "Everyone followed the boat from the shop to the harbor with their vehicles and everyone was clapping," he remembers fondly. "It was just like the Fourth of July Parade. We carried the boat into the water and then rowed away from the town landing with Mark coxing. I'd been lobstering a couple times and I'd been on the ferryboat but other than that I hadn't done a whole lot on the water. It's peaceful being in VIXEN. You can relax and, once you get a rhythm, you don't have to concentrate on rowing."

After talking with Billy I walk back down to the harbor in search of Tiffany Koenig, who also spent her senior year working on VIXEN. She now works for the Bickford Lobster Company on the bait dock. She has her blond hair tucked under a Boston Red Sox baseball cap and chews rhythmically at a wad of gum. As we talk, lobsterboats motor by and there is a strong smell of bait and diesel in the air. On the dock a few men in greasy Levis and rubber boots haul crates of lobsters.

VIXEN'S *launching in 2000 was an island-wide event*

"There's only one girl here and that's me," Tiffany says proudly, pointing at herself with both hands. She is used to this minority position — she was also the only girl involved in the construction of VIXEN. At first she was reluctant to take Mark's class because she found the idea of building a boat intimidating, but now she is proud that a boat she built floats in the harbor. Unfortunately, since graduating, she works seven days a week on the docks, so she doesn't have time to go rowing.

"I love seeing my friends go by in the boat that I helped build and I'd like to keep rowing if I have time — we'll see," Tiffany says, cocking her head trying to imagine how it might be possible.

A few months after rowing with Gigi and the Granite Island Girls I return to Vinalhaven. Encouraged by the success of VIXEN, which was rowed nearly every day during the summer, sometimes twice a day, Mark Jackson and his students have begun the construction of a second gig. Inside the bowed-roof shed, Jackson is dressed in white coveralls and is trying to pick staples out of a jammed staple-gun. While picking, he moves among the students, encouraging them to stay focused on the boat. He hands the revived staple gun to Nicole Laredo, an 18-year-old senior. From a dusty boom box a classic rock station plays Jimi Hendrix while six students work around the focal point of the shed, the hull of the 32-foot gig. The boat is being built upside down and the students are fitting the last of three layers of Spanish cedar over the mold. The staples hold the layers in place while they are being fitted to shape.

Jamie Poole, an 18-year-old with blond hair and a red beard, sits in a gray metal chair next to the heater while prying plywood clamps from the hull. He is familiar with the construction process, having worked on VIXEN last year.

"I hope more schools will build gigs so there could be rowing races between the island schools," says Jamie. He envisions a varsity rowing team that would train regularly and travel to other schools to compete.

While I'm talking to Jamie, Murray Thompson, 19, another of VIXEN's builders, comes into the shop. I had wanted to talk to Murray earlier but it was difficult because of his work schedule. He leaves to go lobstering at 4:30 in the morning and isn't back home until five or six in the evening. Fortunately for me, he didn't go out today because the seas were too rough.

Murray positions himself near the bow of the boat-in-progress and casually rests his back against a shop bench. He often comes up to the school on days when he doesn't go fishing. As he jokes with Jamie and the other students, he sips at a can of Pepsi held lightly in his hand. Murray has his own boat, a Duffy 35 called WHAZZ UP, and goes out lobstering every day he can, even during the winter.

Murray remembers Mark Jackson's technology class as being much different than any schoolwork he had ever done. He liked the concrete goal of having to finish the boat by a certain date.

"I think the launching was the best part," Murray says to me. "A lot of people didn't think we would get the boat done. When we launched it I didn't expect so many people to come out. There must have been over a hundred people."

"Oh, there was more than that," Jamie Poole says, jumping into the conversation while still working on the boat.

"Yeah, must have been more than that," agrees Murray. "Anyway, all the respected townspeople were there."

After my time with the students in the bowed-roof shed, Jackson drives me into town to catch the ferry. I am early so I walk over to Bickford Lobster Company. Tiffany Koenig is still working there, now bundled up for the colder weather. She asks about progress on the new gig — she hasn't had time to go up to the school to see for herself. I talk with Dave Hildings, who is muscling a crate of herring onto a lobsterboat alongside the dock. Dave's son, Nick Hildings, worked on VIXEN last year. Nick was the salutatorian of his class at Vinalhaven School and is now attending Husson College in Bangor. Setting down a heavy crate of bait, Dave gives me Nick's phone number so I can talk to him about VIXEN.

Before going to college, Nick had worked on lobsterboats but the only rowing he had done was out to the mooring in a skiff. "Rowing VIXEN is different from a rowboat because you have a lot of power," says Nick. "You can't see where you are going (the crew faces aft) and so you have to trust the cox."

Nick believes the builders of VIXEN grew to trust each other through the building process. It was necessary to depend on each other to reach the common goal of finishing the boat. In Nick's opinion, VIXEN helps to strengthen the Vinalhaven community by bringing together different groups of people to do something fun. The fact that VIXEN is shared by three or four different groups of rowers with student and adult crews is proof of this cooperative spirit.

Nick is majoring in accounting, a subject he believes the record keeping of lobstering prepared him for, and he doesn't know if he will be able to return to Vinalhaven to pursue his profession. He still comes back to the island when he can and keeps in touch with Mark and the builders of VIXEN. Nick is excited that another gig is being built in the same bowed-roof shed where he built VIXEN. He would advise the younger students to take on the challenge of building a boat. "It pertains to the island and the life out there," explains Nick. "If you're going to live on an island, it's a good thing to know how to build a boat."

***Bruce Halibisky** is a freelance writer and builder of wooden boats living in Rockland, Maine.*

Except where noted, all photographs courtesy of North Haven and Vinalhaven schools – ed.

SACRED SPACE

Long removed, one family leaves its mark

TINA COHEN

Across from my house, through a screen of ancient apple trees, there's a small cemetery. Stones mark the burial of three Pierce family members, whom I assume lived where I live. I have come across fragments from past lives spent where I now spend summers. As I dig in my garden, I have turned up large and small shards of glass, pottery, dishware, and sometimes — intact — small medicinal bottles. A pile of decaying bricks rests under a tangle of wild strawberries. A stone wall crosses the back of our property, and another one snakes through the middle, where it now forms a border of my garden. I have thought of those who worked this same land many years ago, how they also would have nestled their home into the sheltered area where ours now sits, fairly protected from the winds that blow directly off the water.

It is a good place to have a house. There is the Reach to the front of us and Squid Cove and Old Harbor to the side. Sitting on the water's edge, we are treated to tangy salt air and sometimes a punchy fish smell. Fog comes and blends all the boundaries, so that sometimes, we lose sight of where land ends and water begins.

The cemetery measures eight by sixteen feet and has granite posts that would have supported fencing to enclose the space. Black wire has been strung now, inelegantly serving that purpose. Buried in the cemetery are Thomas and Elizabeth Hudson Pierce and one of their sons, James. Curious about them, I visited the Vinalhaven Historical Society to research the family. While there was no one narrative to tell their story, the genealogy I cobbled together provides enticing pieces of the bigger picture.

Thomas and Elizabeth were both born in 1771; Thomas in Boston, his wife in Cohasset on the South Shore below Boston. They married in September, 1791, and in 1794 their first child, Susanna, was born. Where they were living is unclear. Their second child, Josiah, was born one year later and his birthplace is indicated as "Cape Cod." Joseph, the third child, was born in 1797 in Marshfield, Massachusetts, a town also on the South Shore.

When Thomas and Elizabeth moved to Vinalhaven is also unclear. One record, a history of Vinalhaven written for its centennial in 1889, says that Thomas Pierce arrived in 1796. "He was a fisherman, and resided near the Old Harbor." Thomas is listed as a "fisherman" in Vinalhaven censuses; it appears he had that occupation his entire life.

Vinalhaven was first settled in 1765 and incorporated as a town in 1789. By 1800, there were 860 residents in 149 families. There is nothing that clearly indicates why the Pierces decided to relocate to Vinalhaven when they did; where they were living in Massachusetts enabled them to be near family, and Thomas to fish. Perhaps an adventurous spirit and close connections to the fishing communities of Marshfield and Cape Cod influenced their move. Vinalhaven's 1800 census shows that the two largest groups of settlers came from those places.

Josiah, the oldest son, married at age 19 in 1814, a year before his youngest sibling was born. He followed his father into fishing. Married to a young Vinalhaven woman, he had nine children. In 1838, Josiah's wife died and was buried across Old Harbor in the Bay View Cemetery, with a view over the water to the Pierce homestead. Josiah remarried in 1840. A string of deaths in his family followed. A son died in 1844 at age 21 and then, one month later, a son age 18. A married daughter died at age 30 in February 1845, and a son died in March 1845 at 26.

Suffering those losses and others in his extended family, Josiah Pierce seems to have turned to religion. We know that sometime in the 1840s he became a devout Mormon, a member of the Church of Latter-Day Saints that Joseph Smith founded in 1830. His parents joined at some point as well. The church began meeting on Vinalhaven by 1837 with 12 members who had been converted by an itinerant missionary, Wilford Woodruff. An account by him in his 1849 journal mentions the Pierces. He wrote, "We walked 4 miles and stoped [sic] at Br.Josiah Pearce and spent the night. I called upon his Father Thomas Pearce 78 years old. Mother Pearce was also 78 years old this day. Both are members of the Church and strong in the faith. I had a good time with them." Josiah took Woodruff out fishing the next day, and then sailed him across the bay to Camden to continue his travels.

Eventually Josiah moved to Utah, seemingly beckoned by his Mormon faith. He must have gone in the 1850s, possibly after the deaths of his parents. Josiah was buried in Utah in 1867 at the age of 73. We know one of Josiah's children also moved to Utah, married a Mormon woman, and had seven children. There are still Pierces from this branch of the family living there.

The Pierces lost daughter Mary at age 17 in 1818 (she is not buried in the family plot; the location of her grave is not cited). All the other siblings in the Pierce family married here and spent their lives on Vinalhaven. Susanna wed a farmer and had five children. Two are buried next to their parents in the Mills family cemetery. They died in 1845, two months apart, at the ages of 22 and 26.

Joseph, a fisherman, married and had ten children. In 1840, a daughter died at age ten months. In 1849, a son died, lost at sea while fishing. A daughter died at age 22 in 1852. Joseph died two years later. His gravestone, noting him as "Captain" in Carver's Cemetery, is the grandest in the family; the tall granite marker has a carved ship sailing across it, and a poetic inscription.

Patty married a fisherman and had four children. In 1846 their 17-year-old daughter died and in 1853 a 19-year-old son was lost at sea while fishing. Thomas Jr., also a fisherman, married and had six children. Three died as teenagers; Thomas himself died in 1856 when his youngest child was three.

Elizabeth married twice; her second husband left farming in the 1850s for quarry work. It appears she had eight children. A four-year-old daughter died in 1840.

Rachel Boyden Noyes (3)

Hannah married a fisherman and had four children. James married in 1840, at age 31, his bride was 19. No occupation is ever recorded for James. Nine months after their marriage, a son was born and two years later a daughter was born in October 1843. Only two months after that, James died. Isaiah, the youngest and also a fisherman, married and had eight children. I don't know that any of the Pierce families were spared losses, but the records for some are incomplete. Between 1838 and 1849 the Pierces lost at least 15 grandchildren, a son, and a son- and daughter-in-law.

By 1840, Thomas and Elizabeth were again a household of just two. In 1850, Elizabeth was stricken with consumption. She died in February. Thomas lived the last year of his life with his son Joseph and family, until he died in April 1851.

Some questions remain unanswerable. There is no mention of the cause of death for most family members. That there were clusters of deaths at certain times suggests epidemics of disease as the likely culprit. The mortality numbers were common for the time.

No records on Vinalhaven offer further details. After 1851, what was the family's relationship to this place? At some point the dwelling disappeared. When did woods claim the clearing, blackberries blanket the fields, moss envelop the stone walls?

When Wilford Woodruff first visited Vinalhaven in 1837, he wrote a description of the island, including this: "It is a mass of rocks ... The inhabitants get their living entirely by fishing. There is no chance for farming upon the island. There are a few garden patches which are cultivated at great expense. Some few sheep are raised there."

Here where the Pierces once lived, I may have one of those "garden patches" he visited. I like to think the Pierces, if they know I live here now, have welcomed me. I sweat and tire from moving rocks, digging in the dirt and making things grow much as they once did. I pause to feel the breeze, or watch the fog drift, or appreciate the sharp pungent air, as surely they did too. I delight in a salad from my garden, a brilliant lupine in bloom, the perfume of roses by the house. The hard work feels worthwhile. I hope the Pierce family had these small pleasures as well. With no technology, no modern conveniences, they would have worked hard for everything they had. To feed, clothe and shelter a family that large is an effort whose enormity I find mind-boggling. They had left a more civilized, developed part of New England for the wildness but richness of Vinalhaven. I assume they liked it here, found it a good place to build a home and family. Do I feel I share that experience, as a summer person with a summer place? I guess I do. I feel my small acts of homesteading build on their effort, pay tribute to them.

There are no Pierces with that name on the island today; several women have a family connection. While other families dating as far back as the Pierces have stayed and prospered, the Pierces seem to have disappeared. I am very grateful to have around me what makes their presence more tangible — the stone walls, the shards, the cemetery with their names. They are not forgotten; we share this sacred space.

Tina Cohen *is a librarian and archivist at Deerfield Academy, Deerfield, Massachusetts, and a long-time Vinalhaven summer resident.*

The author wishes to thank Esther Bissell and Roy Heisler at the Vinalhaven Historical Society for their warm welcome and knowledgeable assistance.

Island Institute

Supporting the Islands and Communities of the Gulf of Maine

> ***"Islands only survive when people work together."***
>
> — Philip Conkling

Something in each of us is intrigued by the concept of living on an island: a belief in community, perhaps; a sense of quietude; a relationship with nature. In a technology driven world, places where these things flourish are increasingly scarce. At the Island Institute we believe they are worth preserving and celebrating.

Understanding the world from an islander's perspective means recognizing the critical balance between economic life and the natural world. Island and coastal communities depend on the marine environment; without healthy fisheries, they inevitably suffer.

Like an archipelago made up of many islands, the Island Institute has many programs including marine research, community planning, aquaculture, publishing, GIS and remote sensing, scholarships and a highly successful Island Fellows program. Each project, whether on land or at sea, is a vital step in fulfilling the Island Institute's mission as a voice for the balanced future of the islands and waters of the Gulf of Maine.

Christopher Ayres

Island Institute Program Highlights

On Land

- Island Schools Program
- Island Community Planning and Advocacy Support
- Frenchboro Conservation and Community Development Project
- Island Fellows Program
- Publications: books, Working Waterfront/Inter-Island News, Island Journal

At Sea

- Penobscot Bay Research Collaborative
- Atlantic Herring Spawning Project
- Oyster and Mussel Aquaculture
- Lobster Tagging and Recapture Program
- Gulf of Maine Ocean Observing System

Thirty-four percent of the Institute's FY 00-01 operating budget of approximately $3.1 million is expected to come from annual membership dues and from personal and corporate donations, 46 percent from foundations and 20 percent from earned income (publications, retail sales, consultations, service contracts, etc.). The Institute's earned income is substantially greater this year because of a contractual agreement with the National Oceanic and Atmospheric Administration (NOAA) to provide marine-resource research services in Penobscot Bay. The Institute's annual report, listing members and presenting financial details, is available upon request.

Boat Donations

Over the years, the donation of various boats has significantly enhanced our operations. Such gifts have resulted either in boats we keep and use, or boats we can convert into the funds that enable us to maintain our programs. Either way, should you be in a position to consider such a gift, we would very much like to hear from you.

Island Institute

386 Main Street
Rockland, Maine USA 04841
phone (207) 594-9209
fax (207) 594-9314
email <institute@islandinstitute.org>
www.islandinstitute.org

Membership

Membership participation is the only way to sustain a balanced organization, and we welcome your involvement in any capacity. Become a member — call, write or stop in to ask for further details regarding our programs, or become part of our volunteer program.

Planned Giving

Contributing to the Island Institute through a planned giving program can provide a significant tax break for the donor while at the same time sustaining the communities and environment of the Gulf of Maine for years to come. Depending on the nature of the gift, it may generate a better return as a charitable gift than it did as a highly appreciated asset in your portfolio. The Island Institute offers a variety of planned giving options suited to your needs.